Men and Battle
The Men Who Bombed the Reich

THE MEN WHO

A Talisman / Parrish Book

BOMBED THE REICH

Bernard C. Nalty
and Carl Berger

Elsevier-Dutton

New York

D
790
.N 33
1978
June 1998

ISBN: 0-525-93005-1

Published in the United States by E. P. Dutton,
a Division of Sequoia-Elsevier Publishing Company, Inc., New York
Published simultaneously in Canada by
Clarke, Irwin & Company Limited, Toronto and Vancouver

Art Direction: The Etheredges
Production: Stephen Konopka

Printed in the U.S.A.   First Edition
10 9 8 7 6 5 4 3 2 1

Contents

Preface

The focus of this book is the men of the U.S. Eighth Air Force, who flew daylight attacks against Hitler's Germany, braving crippling cold, Luftwaffe fighters and antiaircraft fire. Their efforts formed part of the Combined Bomber Offensive, launched at the Casablanca conference in January 1943 in order to permit "bombing the devils around the clock," the Americans attacking by day and the British by night. After overcoming German defenses, thanks to daylight fighter protection and nighttime electronic aids, the Anglo-American bomber force destroyed a decisive target, the oil industry, and also shattered the enemy's transportation network. Aerial bombardment did not knock Germany out of the war, as its enthusiasts had predicted, but it did contribute substantially to the victory won by Allied arms.

Mr. Carl Berger launched the book, writing drafts of some sections and gathering excerpts from sources before other commitments forced him to withdraw. The transition from one author to another, though far from easy, would have been impossible except for the kindness of several individuals. Major General John W. Huston, Chief of Air Force History, proved especially gracious, as did Dr. John Greenwood, who is preparing a collection of the wartime letters that passed between General Henry H. Arnold and his principal commanders. Lieutenant Colonel Raymond H. Fredette, USAF, Ret., currently at work on a biography of Charles A. Lindbergh, will find several of his splendidly told war stories incorporated in the text. Another Eighth Air Force veteran, Mr. John Corcoran, now with the Office of the Secretary of the Air Force, offered helpful comments on the manuscript. The project would have collapsed, however, had Mr. William Mattson and Mrs. Janet Ball been unwilling or unable to convert rough drafts into legible typescript.

BERNARD C. NALTY

Bombs fall toward a target in the heart of Germany

1. The Mission of Ruthie II

On 28 July 1943, 302 American bombers circled over England until their formations had taken shape, then headed into Europe. Part of the force shaped a course for Kassel, Germany, where, as it turned out, bad weather prevented accurate bombing. The other feinted toward Hamburg, a frequent target of both British and American raiders, then continued inland toward Oschersleben, 90 miles southwest of Berlin. This was the deepest penetration of Germany yet attempted by the U.S. Eighth Air Force, and the target seemed worth the effort, for the planes were to bomb a factory that produced one of Germany's deadliest fighters, the Focke-Wulf FW 190. When the B-17s arrived, heavy cloud shrouded Oschersleben, but the lead bombardier found a small hole in the overcast, recognized a crossroads a few miles from the aiming point, and dropped his bombs squarely on the aircraft plant. The other bombardiers used these explosions as a guide.

Piloting one of the B-17s, *Ruthie II*, was First Lieutenant Robert L. Campbell, who had named the plane after his wife. The copilot was

Flight Officer John C. Morgan, a veteran of the Royal Canadian Air Force, who had once managed a pineapple plantation in the Fiji Islands, besides working as a salesman in his native Texas. Morgan took the controls after takeoff, turning them back to Campbell about a quarter of an hour's flying time from the German coast.

The pilot had barely taken over when a group of enemy fighters attacked. On the first pass the Germans managed to knock out the oxygen system supplying gunners in the waist, tail and radio compartment. Moments later other fighters came out of the sun at 2 o'clock, the right front, firing 20-mm shells and machine gun bullets through the windscreen on the copilot's side of the cabin. One shell split Campbell's skull, an ultimately mortal wound that left him unconscious. The pilot slumped forward over the control wheel, wrapping both arms around it and forcing the airplane into a shallow dive.

Morgan immediately pulled back on the wheel on his side of the cockpit. He tried instinctively to regain his place in the formation so that *Ruthie II* would not become easy prey for the Germans. As he struggled against Campbell's weight on the controls, the copilot called to the crew for help, only to discover that the interphone system had been knocked out.

Ground personnel on the lookout at a bomber base

The Focke-Wulf factory was just 25 miles distant when the top turret gunner, Sergeant Tyle Weaver, came staggering into the cabin. A 20-mm shell had penetrated the plexiglas turret, tearing off an arm near the socket, and knocking him onto the deck of the control compartment. Gushing blood and barely conscious, the sergeant gestured for Morgan to take the bomber down, then fell forward through the opening that led to the navigator's compartment, where Second Lieutenant Keith Koske tried unsuccessfully to stanch the flow of blood. In desperation, Koske helped Weaver into a parachute, opened the hatch in the floor and pushed him from the plane.

Although Morgan could not know this, the waist and tail gunners and the radio operator had by now passed out from lack of oxygen. Since he no longer heard their guns firing, the flight officer assumed they had bailed out, a further argument against breaking formation, even though he could barely see the other bombers. Wind roared through the shattered plexiglas, blinding him if he tried to look straight ahead; he could see only through the overhead and side windows.

The thought of pushing the bail-out alarm was tempting, but the nose gun still was firing, which indicated that the bombardier as well as the navigator remained unhurt. The bombs were still on board, and the target was close at hand. If he could overcome the pressure exerted on the controls by the dying pilot, he could stay with the formation, bomb the target and return safely to England.

For two hours Morgan did the impossible, keeping the bomber in formation with his right hand while using his left arm to hold the fatally injured pilot away from the control column. He flew *Ruthie II* the rest of the way to the factory, guided the plane through the bomb run and headed eventually across the North Sea toward safety. During this ordeal, Morgan had to take evasive action whenever fighters closed on the B-17's unprotected tail, then advance the throttles and regain his assigned place.

Over the North Sea, Koske emerged from his compartment, discovered the exhausted Morgan, and slid Campbell into the nose of the plane where the bombardier held the dying pilot to keep him from falling from the hatch through which Weaver had parachuted. The flight officer no longer had to wrestle the controls as he brought *Ruthie II* across the English coast. All the gasoline gauges registered empty, since cannon fire had punched holes in the tanks and precious fuel had drained away.

4

At the first airfield the weary fliers saw, their calls to the control tower went unanswered; *Ruthie II*'s radio transmitter had failed. Morgan, however, had no choice but to enter the landing pattern. With the help of the tail gunner, who had recovered consciousness and now lowered the flaps and landing gear, he landed the plane safely. The mission to Oschersleben was ended, and for his heroism that day Morgan received the Medal of Honor, the nation's highest award for gallantry.

Incredibly, Sergeant Weaver survived his parachute jump, was taken to a German hospital and lived despite the grievous loss of blood. The gunners who had lain unconscious, or nearly so, for hours also survived though they suffered severe frostbite. And, ironically, on a subsequent mission over Germany, Morgan was shot down, taken prisoner and confined for the remainder of the war.

Seriously wounded gunner is rushed to an ambulance

2. The Daylight Challenge

The Oschersleben raid, during which Campbell died and Morgan earned the Medal of Honor, was the kind of strategic mission, a precision attack on an important industrial plant, that the leaders of the U.S. Army Air Forces believed would defeat Germany. Inspired by Billy Mitchell, a brigadier general during World War I and afterward a masterly propagandist for air power, these men had borrowed freely from foreign bomber enthusiasts. For example, they frequently cited an Italian, Giulio Douhet, who predicted that aerial bombing could paralyze a nation's economy and destroy its will to resist. Another influential foreigner was Hugh ("Boom") Trenchard, for 10 years Britain's Chief of Air Staff, who believed that only the bomber could "attack the enemy, force him to fight, and . . . defeat him." But the Americans honored Trenchard as the champion of the independent air force, which they hoped the Army Air Corps would become, rather than as a proponent of bombardment.

In the United Kingdom, however, Trenchard found ample support

7

The B-17 Fortress seemed almost invincible

for his emphasis on bombing. Memories of the World War I zeppelin raids and the more destructive attacks by lumbering multiengine airplanes died hard, so that during the 1920s the Royal Air Force became fascinated with the possibility of doing to German cities what the enemy had done to London in the recent war. Trenchard and younger disciples like Arthur Harris came to believe that air power could defeat an enemy, even though the hostile army remained intact. Never again, if they were correct, would a British expeditionary force have to deploy to the Continent and fight a seemingly endless series of bloody but inconclusive battles. Instead, the bomber would shatter the enemy, not through indiscriminately terrorizing civilians but by terrorizing precisely those workers whose efforts were essential to the war effort.

The U.S. Army Air Corps cultivated its own theory of bombing, partly devised from foreign sources and partially homegrown. The doctrine emerged from the Air Corps Tactical School at Maxwell Field, Ala. where, during the early 1930s, interest centered upon aerial bombardment. Air Corps officers, many of whom rose to high command during World War II, proposed a form of strategic bombing that was to be capable of defeating an enemy by attacking his entire war-making potential—political, social and economic—rather than simply his military forces. At this time, however, the Air Corps lacked both the equipment and the measure of independence from Army control essential for conducting this kind of war.

Equipment proved easier to obtain than autonomy. The first item acquired by the air arm was a bombsight. Observers attending U.S. Navy bombing experiments in the fall of 1931 marveled at the accuracy of a gyrostabilized optical device invented by C. L. Norden, who had been supplying bombsights to the Navy for over a decade. The Air Corps purchased its first Norden sights during the following year, and the new piece of equipment was soon achieving spectacular results in the bright sunshine and calm air of the southwestern desert. On these cloudless bombing ranges was born the legend that a bombardier using the Norden sight could hit a pickle barrel from 10,000 feet.

Next came the airplane, the Boeing B-17. Although touted as a weapon for coastal defense to placate isolationist public opinion, this was actually the fast, heavily armed, long-range bomber needed to conduct strategic bombing. By the standards of the mid-1930s, the new bomber seemed almost invincible. In theory, at least, no enemy could withstand daylight precision bombing by massed formations of B-17s fitted with the Norden sight.

Sir Arthur Harris (standing, 1.) believed in heavy area attacks

As the clouds of war gathered in Europe, President Franklin D. Roosevelt repeatedly called for the expansion of the Army Air Corps. During the three years ending in December 1941, this branch of service received authorization to spend some $8 billion to purchase almost 38,000 airplanes. In production, in at least small quantities, by the time the Japanese attacked Pearl Harbor were all but one of the aircraft that bore the brunt of the air war against Germany. The sole exception was the North American P-51 Mustang fighter.

Since details of aircraft design would have to change to meet the evolving demands of modern war, the Air Corps sent observers to France and Great Britain to report on both equipment and tactics. By February 1940 the American air arm was planning to install armor, self-sealing fuel tanks and additional guns in the B-17 and other aircraft.

Although assured of money and equipment, military airmen did not receive the autonomy they desired. A reorganization that went into effect in June 1941 did, however, mark a long stride along the road to independence. The Army Air Forces came into existence, subordinate to the Army Chief of Staff, General George C. Marshall, but possessing a staff of its own and coequal with Army Field Forces, the corps areas in the United States, the overseas establishments, the chiefs of the combat arms and the administrative bureaus. Chosen to command the reorganized air arm was Major General Henry H. ("Hap") Arnold.

One of the first activities undertaken by the staff of Army Air Forces was the preparation of an air annex to a war plan based upon the realistic assumption that the United States would become involved in a two-front war against Germany and Japan. The overall plan further suggested that the United States remain on the defensive in the Pacific until Germany was defeated, then crush Japan. Most of the work on the air annex fell to four officers—Lieutenant Colonel Harold L. George, who was chief of General Arnold's Air War Plans Division; Lieutenant Colonel Kenneth Walker; Major Laurence S. Kuter; and Major Haywood S. Hansell, Jr. Aware that any plan presented by his division would require Army approval, George avoided alienating the ground generals. Instead of claiming bluntly that a bombing offensive would defeat Germany without the assistance of military or naval forces, he described his concept as an air offensive designed to prepare Europe for an amphibious invasion followed by a land campaign. He did suggest, however, that bombing itself might possibly persuade the Germans to surrender.

10

The air annex called for attacks upon three elements of Germany's economy that seemed essential for waging modern war. These "primary air objectives" were disruption of the German electric power grid, disruption of the transportation net and destruction of the synthetic oil and petroleum refining industry. To accomplish these goals would, of course, require neutralization of the German air force—the Luftwaffe—especially the fighter arm, principally by bombing aircraft plants, engine factories and airfields.

George and his colleagues believed that they could pave the way for invasion—or, preferably, force Germany to surrender—by destroying 154 targets in the three main categories of electricity, transportation and fuel. Unfortunately, most of these generators, rail yards and refineries could be repaired quickly and would have to undergo repeated attack, a difficult task because of the weather in the British Isles, where most of the attacks on Germany would originate. Cloud or fog might reduce the number of bombing days to as few as five out of 30. An air offensive of this magnitude would obviously erode civilian morale, but George and the others opposed attacks designed solely for moral effect until Germany tottered on the brink of surrender.

The proposed air annex moved serenely through the channels of command until both General Marshall and Secretary of War Henry L. Stimson had endorsed it. The final step was to explain the concept to President Roosevelt, but on 7 December 1941, before this briefing could take place, the Japanese attacked Pearl Harbor. The emergency described in the basic plan had become reality with stunning swiftness.

While American airmen dealt with concepts, selecting targets for airplanes not yet built, the Royal Air Force Bomber Command had subjected its doctrines to the test of combat. At first the British had dispatched their Vickers Wellingtons on unescorted daylight raids, but German fighters avoided the power turrets installed fore and aft, attacked from the beam and shot down 20 of the twin-engine planes in four unsuccessful raids. Meanwhile, Armstrong Whitworth Whitleys were plodding unchallenged through the night to drop propaganda leaflets on German cities. Deterred for a time by fear of provoking a superior force of enemy bombers, the RAF did not launch a real air offensive until after the German invasion of France in the spring of 1940. Because of the comparative immunity of the Whitleys, these attacks took place at night.

The officers and men of Bomber Command believed their efforts were effective. Directed to bomb oil refineries and synthetic fuel plants, crews consistently reported finding their assigned objectives and starting fires with their bombs. An intelligence estimate circulated late in 1940 claimed that fewer than 550 tons of explosives dropped on the factories after dark had reduced the output of synthetic oil by some 15 percent. In short, Sir Charles Portal and the men of Bomber Command had succeeded in convincing themselves that they were conducting precision bombing by moonlight.

To British eyes, however, precision was becoming less important, especially after the Luftwaffe destroyed the industrial city of Coventry in November 1940. Sir Richard Peirse, who had taken over from Portal on the latter's appointment as Chief of Air Staff, stepped up the oil attacks, while still finding opportunities to attack other targets and to avenge Coventry by bombing out the center of Mannheim, Germany.

In the summer of 1941, Lord Cherwell, science adviser to Prime Minister Winston Churchill, sponsored a dispassionate review of the effectiveness of night bombing. On the basis of some 600 aerial photographs taken during June and July, the review panel concluded that only one bomber in 10 found its target, let alone bombed it accurately. As a result, the scientist pushed the development of navigation aids to guide bombers to their objectives. Significantly, despite these findings Bomber Command did not resurrect the practice of daylight bombing.

Sir Arthur Harris took over Bomber Command in February 1942 and promptly abandoned any pretense at precision bombardment. He reaped the technological harvest sown by Lord Cherwell, including a navigational beam, received by equipment on board the bombers, that kept the aircraft on course at least part way to the objective. Not every bomber, however, had to carry the device, for Harris used his most experienced crews as pathfinders to find the target, usually the center of a large city, and mark it with incendiaries. Other bombers followed in a loose stream, instead of the compact formation favored by the Americans, and used the blaze as an aiming point for their bombs.

On 8 March, Harris tested these tactics against Essen. He followed this successful raid with a devastating attack on the Baltic port of Lübeck, a raid that marked the combat debut of the new four-engine Avro Lancaster bomber. On this night, the massive slab-sided Lancasters devoted most of their bomb capacity, a maximum of nine tons, to incendiaries, which gutted the center of the city, an area containing many wooden structures dating from medieval times. These buildings burned like tinder, and the spreading flames consumed almost half the town, destroying some 2,000 homes, factories and an electric power plant, besides the cathedral and a bank.

After a disappointing start, Bomber Command seemed to have discovered a means of carrying the war to the enemy. Thanks to the new navigation aid, called Gee, and the specially trained pathfinder force, Bomber Command could attain the accuracy necessary for "city busting." This kind of raid, according to Lord Cherwell, had a bonus effect— it drove German families from their homes, increasing the strain on the fabric of the nation's society. As a result, the scientist proposed a list of 58 large cities whose destruction would leave a third of the German people homeless.

While Bomber Command was acquiring the aircraft, bombing technique and navigation aids needed for successful night area bombing, the American Eighth Air Force was organizing for the express purpose of flying daylight precision attacks from British bases against Germany. On 28 January, a little less than two months after the United States and Great Britain had become allies in World War II, the Eighth Air Force came into being. Brigadier General Asa H. Duncan assumed command of a skeletal headquarters at the National Guard armory in Savannah, Ga. His organization consisted of 74 officers and 81 enlisted men. Duncan himself was one of four experienced pilots in the headquarters. The other veteran airmen were Colonel Leon W. Johnson, who would earn the Medal of Honor, Colonel P. L. Williams and Major Charles Jones.

Three days after Duncan took command, General Arnold selected Brigadier General Ira C. Eaker as Bomber Commander, Eighth Air Force, Army Air Forces in Great Britain. Eaker was the youngest member of perhaps the most celebrated trio in the old Air Corps, frequently sharing the spotlight with Hap Arnold and Carl A. Spaatz. Eaker and Spaatz, for instance, had taken part in the flight of the *Question Mark*, establishing an aerial endurance record thanks, in part, to midair refueling. Arnold had not only commanded a massed flight of B-10 bombers from Washington, D.C., to Alaska and back but had written popular books on aviation, in collaboration with Eaker, and commanded both the Air Corps and its successor, the Army Air Forces.

Eaker and six other officers, wearing civilian clothes, left LaGuardia Field, New York City, on 4 February, on the first leg of their flight to London. The party included Lieutenant Colonel Frank A. Armstrong, Jr., Major Peter Beasley, Captain Beirne Lay, Jr., Captain Frederick

General Eaker (center) inspects bomb damage

"Pinetree"—the famous Eighth Air Force headquarters near London

W. Castle, who would be awarded his Medal of Honor posthumously, First Lieutenant Harris B. Hull and Second Lieutenant William S. Cowart, Jr. Bad weather delayed the flight, which did not reach London until 20 February, after stops in Bermuda and at Lisbon. On the flight from Lisbon to London, the Americans sighted a twin-engine midwing monoplane, believed to be a German fighter, which crossed their course ahead and slightly above the transport. The intruder seemed to be trailing smoke from one engine. Since the Nazis had a web of intelligence agents throughout Portugal, the possibility occurred to Eaker that this plane had been sent to intercept the airliner but had been unable to attack because of engine trouble.

Other officers joined Eaker in England until the strength of his bomber headquarters reached 19. But he still had no planes, no crews and no maintenance men. The staff set up living quarters and offices at Royal Air Force Bomber Command headquarters near High Wycombe, a small industrial town in Buckinghamshire, 29 miles west of London, where the Eighth Air Force later would establish its command post. From High Wycombe, Eaker and his staff addressed the gigantic task of preparing to receive the men and planes of the Eighth Air Force and commit them against the common foe.

In May 1942, Major General Carl Spaatz became Commanding General, Eighth Air Force, though he had not yet left the United States, and Eaker remained in charge of the organization's advance echelon in Great Britain. Meanwhile, British authorities had closed a girls' boarding school at High Wycombe and made it available to Eaker as his headquarters. This placed the command elements of the Eighth Air Force in Britain and the RAF just four or five miles apart, a proximity that reflected the close cooperation between the two organizations.

American officers made frequent trips to various RAF headquarters, airfields and supply depots, discussing British procedures and working long hours on reports for the future guidance of the Eighth Air Force. Although the Eighth was a completely new air force without an hour's operational experience, it had at its disposal the knowledge gained by the RAF in more than two and a half years of aerial warfare against the Axis powers. During this early period of preparation and planning, Eaker and his fellow officers flew throughout the United Kingdom in a borrowed training plane, the British version of the two-place North American AT-6, the only plane available to the Eighth Air Force at the time.

15

Eaker, Sir Arthur Harris and Harris's wife, Lady Julia, became such close friends that while the American general's quarters were being completed at High Wycombe, he moved in with the Harrises. One night, as Eaker dined at the Harris home, he learned that Lady Jill had prepared a birthday party for the air marshal. Eaker remarked that it was his own birthday and found himself being feted in a double celebration.

Although some American officers felt awkward at teas or banquets, Eaker adapted instantly, exuding a charm and courtesy that impressed both British airmen and civilians. For example, in June 1942, at a ball given by the lord mayor of High Wycombe, where his headquarters was located, Eaker responded to an invitation to speak. His talk was brief and to the point, containing just 21 words: "We won't do much talking until we've done more fighting. We hope that when we leave you'll be glad we came." He then sat down.

The two senior officers, Eaker and Harris, respected each other's views on bombing. Although Harris would have preferred to divert the first few hundred B-17s to antisubmarine reconnaissance or use them for night attack, he refrained from pressing the point, preferring to show Eaker pictures of the damage done by nighttime city busting. The air marshal realized that Eaker had to get his bombers into action as quickly as possible, or the planes might be sent to the Pacific; no time could be lost retraining men and refitting planes for operating in darkness. Harris curbed his doubts, and Eaker avoided rash promises of what daylight attack could do, keeping in mind what he had said at the lord mayor's ball—the British had bombed Germany, the Americans had not.

By 31 July the number of American combat aircraft based in the British Isles had grown to 423, but the press and public were just beginning to understand the kind of war the organization would wage. During the previous month, in an off-the-record press conference held shortly after his arrival in England, General Spaatz had caused considerable astonishment by casually admitting that the Eighth Air Force remained "interested" in daylight bombing, even though both Bomber Command and the Luftwaffe had shifted to night operations because of the unbearably heavy losses suffered during the day.

When the public became aware that Spaatz was determined to bomb by daylight, doubts surfaced in the press. A leading British journalist declared that the B-17 and B-24, though they were doing useful work for Coastal Command flying antisubmarine and shipping patrols, were not suited to aerial combat over the continent of Europe. It was a great pity, he suggested, that the U.S. Army Air Forces and the vast American aircraft industry had committed their great potential to daytime bombardment, for they could have built new Lancasters, Britain's finest heavy bombers, and trained crews to fly them by night. Instead of returning to a discredited theory, the Americans could have lent their undeniable strength to the execution of proven tactics.

In the face of these comments, Spaatz, Eaker and their American colleagues sought to lend substance to their vision of a huge air force capable of leveling German industry, perhaps forcing Hitler to surrender before the first soldiers set foot on European soil. While they worked, Harris stood quietly by, willing to give his allies a chance. If daylight bombing failed, and British experience indicated it would, the Americans might be persuaded to change their plans. As a result, Spaatz and Eaker launched their daytime offensive under the questioning gaze of their British comrades.

B-17s on a daylight mission over Europe

③.Men and Bombers

The rock upon which the American theory of daylight precision bombing rested was the Boeing B-17 Flying Fortress, equipped with the Norden optical bombsight. When the Eighth Air Force began gathering strength for operations against Germany, the basic design of the Flying Fortress was roughly eight years old. During the summer of 1934, while the Boeing Airplane Company was working on an experimental aerial dreadnought that became the XB-15, the War Department held a competition for an operational multiengine bomber capable of carrying a ton of bombs 2,000 miles at a speed of 200 miles per hour. Although Boeing's competitors offered twin-engine designs, Clairmont Egtvedt, one of the firm's vice presidents, insisted upon applying lessons learned in the early stages of the XB-15 project to create a slightly smaller four-engine craft that would nevertheless dwarf the standard bomber of that era, the Martin B-10. Assigned to the new undertaking, Boeing Model 299, were two young engineers, Edward Wells and E. G. Emery, to whom the company entrusted more than a quarter of a million dollars.

General "Hap" Arnold with
General Omar Bradley

In August 1935, Model 299, the prototype of the B-17, rolled out of the Boeing plant at Seattle. The gleaming cylindrical fuselage measured 69 feet from a bulbous plexiglas gun compartment at the nose to the pointed tail cone. The thick wings extended 103 feet from tip to tip, with nacelles jutting from the leading edge to house the four Wright Cyclone radial engines. Tradition has it that a reporter looked at the beautifully streamlined airplane, with its five glassed-in gun positions, and christened it the Flying Fortress.

En route to Wright Field, Dayton, Ohio, for testing by the Army Air Corps, Model 299 averaged 232 miles per hour, arriving about two hours ahead of schedule. Triumph soon gave way to tragedy, however, for in October, after several successful flights, the huge bomber crashed immediately after takeoff, killing two of the five men on board. An investigation disclosed that an oversight had caused the fatal wreck. Someone had failed to remove a wooden block that locked the rudder while the plane was parked, to prevent damage from wind gusts.

The War Department then placed an order with Boeing, but for only 13 of the aircraft, barely enough to keep the firm in business. In contrast, Douglas Aircraft received an order for 133 twin-engine B-18s, slower, shorter range but much cheaper than the Y1B-17, military designation of the new Boeing. Although the Army had not yet accepted the principle of strategic bombardment, it had given the big bomber enthusiasts—officers like Henry H. Arnold, Hugh Knerr and Kenneth Walker—an opportunity to test their theories.

20

Test them they did, with a series of flights that both caught the imagination of the American people and demonstrated the superiority of the four-engine bomber over its less expensive rivals. Lieutenant Colonel Robert C. Olds, for instance, set a transcontinental speed record and later led six of the Y1B-17s on a goodwill flight to Buenos Aires. Curtis E. LeMay, a navigator on the South American tour, later plotted a course that enabled three of the bombers, again commanded by Olds, to intercept an ocean liner 700 miles at sea.

Although in need of improvement, such as the addition of superchargers to permit bombing from the substratosphere, these first B-17s were extremely rugged, a trait inherited by later models. Over Langley Field, Va., Lieutenant William Bentley wandered into a thunderhead and encountered an updraft that threw the plane onto its back. Before he could regain control, the Flying Fortress had righted itself and then slipped into a spin. These maneuvers imposed strains far in excess of designed strength, but the only damage consisted of popped rivets and wrinkled aluminum skin. The B-17 would later prove as resistant to battle damage as it had to the fury of the storm.

After the outbreak of war in Europe, which resulted in an increase in B-17 production, the United States agreed to provide 20 B-17Cs to Britain's Royal Air Force. This was a transitional model with larger engines than earlier types, turbosuperchargers and additional hand-operated machine guns. About to start down the assembly line was the improved E version with two power-operated gun turrets and twin .50-caliber weapons in the tail.

The high-wing B-24 Liberator

When the British sent their Cs, called Fortress Is, into battle, the results were disastrous. Bomber Command could dispatch no more than a handful of the inadequately armed Fortresses at any one time, too few to defend themselves or to lay down a destructive pattern with the eight 600-pound bombs that each one carried. RAF crews, moreover, were unused to high-altitude flying, and the American bombsight they had received was less accurate than the secret Norden type reserved for Air Corps Fortresses. Although hundreds of improved B-17s were leaving factories in the United States, the British had not only lost interest in this type of aircraft but had come to doubt the American scheme of precision daylight bombing by formations of aircraft capable of defending themselves against fighter attack.

Another four-engine bomber was entering service along with these new B-17s. This was the Consolidated B-24 Liberator, designed under the supervision of Isaac M. Laddon, which flew for the first time in December 1939. A slab-sided, high-wing monoplane with twin rudders, the B-24 looked ugly in comparison to the graceful B-17. The Liberator's tricycle landing gear imparted a swaying motion as the plane taxied, and this nautical roll, plus the plane's resemblance to one of the sea-planes that Consolidated Aircraft built for the U.S. Navy, inspired Fortress crews to refer to the B-24 as the Banana Boat.

The early Liberators, however, profited from the "Davis wing," which enabled them to fly higher and farther than the Flying Fortress. Patented by David R. Davis, this wing combined great length with narrow chord, providing a high aspect ratio that permitted efficient operation at high altitude. The altitude advantage diminished as Consolidated engineers installed additional gun turrets and other equipment on their bomber, so that by the end of the war in Europe the Liberators usually bombed from a lower altitude than the B-17s. Even so, the B-24 could carry a heavier bomb load farther than the Flying Fortress. A typical B-17 mission involved a round trip of 1,200 to 1,400 miles to drop 4,000 or 5,000 pounds of bombs, whereas a Liberator could carry more than a ton of explosives 1,200 miles, attack the target, and return to its base. Or, over shorter distances, the Consolidated bomber could carry as much as six tons of bombs.

The Davis wing had its drawbacks, however, for it was intended for high-speed flight at high altitude. At slow speeds the wing tended to stall during abrupt turns. Also, the combination of narrow wing chord and comparatively long fuselage caused the plane to "porpoise" if power settings changed suddenly: if the pilot increased power, the nose tended to drop, and when he throttled back the nose came up. Maintaining formation required smooth coordination and a steady hand.

Both the Flying Fortress and the Liberator cruised at about 170 miles per hour and had top speeds slightly in excess of 300 miles per hour. The B-17G, the most modern of that type, carried thirteen .50-caliber guns, six of them in power turrets, compared with the five manually operated .30-caliber or .50-caliber weapons planned for the original Model 299. Similarly, later-model B-24s carred ten .50-caliber guns, eight of them in power turrets, instead of the original armament of three .50-caliber and four .30-caliber machine guns.

If the Liberator had the advantage of greater range and bomb capacity, the Flying Fortress enjoyed the reputation of being more ruggedly built. Those who flew the B-17 testified to the damage it could survive; one of the Gs, for example, limped from Hungary to its base in Italy with a jagged hole four feet in diameter in each side of the fuselage aft of the waist gun positions. Ira C. Eaker, who attained the rank of lieutenant general while commanding the Eighth Air Force, maintained that the B-17 was "a bit more rugged" than the B-24, and Curtis LeMay, who led the 4th Bombardment Wing against Regensburg in August 1943, declared that the Flying Fortress was "as tough an airplane as was ever built."

Whether flying the Liberator or the B-17, a 10-man air crew—consisting of pilot, copilot, bombardier, navigator, radio operator and gunners—underwent similar experiences. Their day began with a briefing that disclosed the target and route, information inscribed on a large map covered by a cloth. As the covering was drawn aside, sometimes confirming rumors that had circulated for days, the crews calculated how deeply they would have to penetrate the defenses of Germany and estimated their chances of survival. Instead of the hoped-for milk run to Aachen or Wilhelmshaven, the target might be Schweinfurt or even Berlin. As dozens of simultaneous briefings were taking place at the American airfields in East Anglia, weather reconnaissance planes made a last-minute check of the target and its alternate.

At midmorning the crews, wearing their clumsy flight gear and carrying parachutes, entered their bomb-laden aircraft; soon, at a dozen or more bases, the raiders began taking off. As they climbed to the assigned altitude, pilots watched for the brightly painted airplanes, usually obsolete bombers, upon which they assembled, forming combat wings of

Briefing officer outlines mission to Eighth
Air Force bomber crews

54 to 63 planes; in the spring of 1943 wings normally consisted of three combat boxes of 18 to 21 bombers. In the case of B-17s, which generally flew slightly higher than Liberators, the lead plane in the lead box flew at 25,000 feet, with another box centered at 26,000 feet and a third at 24,000 feet. Within each box were three squadrons, the center squadron in the lead, a second echeloned high and to the right, and a third below and to the left. Formations, like bombing altitudes, changed during the war to keep pace with changing German defenses.

Assembly required precise flying in the best of weather, with hundreds of aircraft taking their positions in the same general area, but fog or cloud cover could turn the procedure into a nightmare. The bombers groped toward the prescribed altitude and assembly point, relying on the aircraft instruments and a radio beacon that marked the rendezvous. Since they had taken off just minutes apart, the slightest miscalculation could result in a midair collision. While a colonel in command of the 4th Bombardment Wing, LeMay had insisted that his pilots practice instrument flying, and he prided himself on their ability to take off, organize their formations and head for Europe while other units were waiting on the ground for the fog to lift. LeMay's men did benefit, however, from slightly better weather, on the average, than was experienced at some of the other English airfields.

A four- to six-hour mission in the substratosphere was a physical and mental ordeal for those who took part. The interior of a B-17 was cramped, constricting the movement of men encumbered by heavy fleece-lined clothing and tethered by tubes to oxygen bottles. Even in the roomier B-24, crew members complained that they could scarcely move about in the "teddy-bear suits."

The combination of tight quarters and bulky clothing kept most crewmen from wearing seat-pack parachutes. When the bail-out alarm rang, the gunners and sometimes other individuals had to leave their posts, clip on parachutes hung inside the fuselage and jump through an exit hatch. If the plane remained stable, escape was possible, but if the bomber fell into a spin, the resulting rotational forces could pin the men helpless inside the fuselage.

At bombing altitude, with air rushing through the open waist gun positions, the temperature was 50 degrees below zero. Some of the men, such as the waist gunners, wore electrically heated boots and gloves, but sudden movement easily snapped the wires that carried current. Frostbite, painfully frozen extremities and faces, occurred on almost every mission, especially among those who suffered wounds that required the loosening or removal of clothing. Anyone unlucky enough to be wearing damp clothes was certain to incur frostbite, and the moisture might result from perspiration, from being caught in the rain before takeoff or from having to urinate in the midst of an air battle, when there was no opportunity to use an ammunition can. Even worse, the rubber bladder of the standard oxygen mask might freeze at altitudes above 20,000 feet, causing unconsciousness and possibly death.

The cold hampered emergency activity, whether clearing a jammed gun or administering first aid. In either case, the airman almost always had to remove a glove, risking injury from frostbite or freezing. A hot machine gun cooled so quickly that within a few minutes bare fingers would freeze to the metal.

The most frightening aspect of a bomber mission probably was the helplessness felt at some time by almost everyone on board the big planes. Seeing their aircraft as part of a huge formation that nevertheless seemed isolated in the vastness of the sky, the individual men felt them-

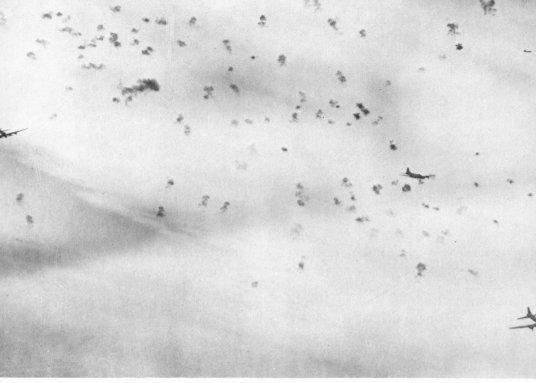

Antiaircraft fire seeks out a B-17 formation

selves being propelled deep into Germany by forces beyond their control. Carpets of bursting shells spread out before them, and occasionally
a nearby B-17 or B-24 dissolved in flame as the guns scored a direct hit.
German fighters swarmed all around them, firing rockets to break up
the formation or rolling in to attack with cannon and machine guns. The
pilot and copilot of many a bomber, especially the older models with
only hand-operated weapons firing forward, sought the illusory protection of the control panel as a Messerschmitt or Focke-Wulf approached
head-on, trailing smoke from its guns. On board the bombers there was
no place to hide, no cover except for the armor built into the plane. Not
until late in the war did the introduction of body armor provide some
measure of additional protection.

Despite cold, discomfort and danger, pilots had to keep their place
in formation, and gunners had to recognize the enemy immediately,
track him and fire without squandering the limited supply of ammunition. Pressures were especially heavy on lead navigators and lead bombardiers, who had to bring their unit to the objective and place its

bombs on target. Unexpected cloud cover or shifting wind could frustrate the best of navigators, for one German town obscured by cloud or haze could easily be mistaken for another. Nor could the Norden bombsight penetrate cloud or see through smoke from fires started by groups that had already dropped their bombs.

Smoke and dust raised by the earlier squadrons sometimes caused later units to bomb inaccurately. Merely hitting the source of the smoke did not ensure accuracy, for wind could distend the cloud, and if bombs missed the mark, the pattern of fires and explosions became distorted. Though it was small consolation to the Americans, the British had similar problems at night, as the original target markers disappeared in a sea of flame.

Fatigue and danger took their toll. To conceal his fears, a man might become unnaturally loud, argue with his fellow airmen and engage in drunken fights, or he might keep strictly to himself, counting the number of missions he had yet to survive before his combat tour came to an end. Fortunately, aircraft maintenance and bad weather provided frequent respite from the air war, enabling the crews to visit nearby towns and meet British women.

Yet there were those who broke under the strain, men who could no longer force themselves into an airplane. Occasionally collapse occurred after a single mission during which, for instance, the individual might have watched helplessly as a friend bled to death. Another person might fly several dangerous strikes before reaching the breaking point, his own crisis the result of cumulative tension, though possibly triggered by a single incident such as being trapped inside a gun turret and believing the plane was going down. Statistics revealed that only 2 percent of those flying bomber missions during the summer of 1943 became psychiatric casualties, either temporary or permanent. In human terms, however, this represented two persons from the combined crews of 10 bombers.

In his autobiography, Curtis LeMay revealed his conflicting views about combat fatigue, as this form of disability was called. Instinct told him that once a man got into the airplane, he would be all right, but experience proved otherwise. Nor could LeMay dismiss those who balked at combat as weak or cowardly, for some of them had backgrounds, character and interests much like his own. He had to concede that some men, however courageous or determined, could push themselves to a point where the body rebelled against commands from the will. Getting into the airplane was not always the answer; rest or other treatment might be necessary, a temporary transfer to noncombat duty, or in rare instances reassignment to a different type of combat aircraft.

All sorts of individuals served in the daylight bomber offensive. Few of them looked less like a soldier than Maynard ("Snuffy") Smith, who served as a belly gunner in a B-17 flown by First Lieutenant Lewis Johnson. On Smith's first mission, an attack on St. Nazaire, a French port, Smith's turret went out of operation. He got the hatch open, climbed into the smoke-filled interior of the fuselage and saw the waist gunners preparing to bail out. Instead of snapping on his parachute and following their example, he chose to stay with the aircraft and battle a fire being fed by escaping oxygen. After emptying every extinguisher on board, he put out the flames, then triumphantly urinated on the embers. He somehow managed to drag the wounded tail gunner to the comparative safety of the plane's waist and gave him first aid. When not fighting the blaze or ministering to his wounded fellow crewman, Smith manned one or the other of the waist guns to keep German fighters at bay. These exploits earned Smith the Medal of Honor, and upon receiving this award, he proved as persuasive as he had been heroic, arguing successfully that as the holder of the nation's highest award for gallantry he should not have to risk his life on other combat missions.

An opposite to Smith in military bearing and background was Lieutenant Colonel Leon Vance, a graduate of the U.S. Military Academy. Although not at the controls, Vance commanded a B-24 which took three hits from antiaircraft fire while approaching its target in France. Shell fragments had almost severed his foot, but the aircraft commander remained fully conscious and ordered the pilot to complete the bomb run, then head for England. Near the Channel coast, he realized that the battered Liberator was doomed and told the crew to bail out, only to discover that one man was too badly wounded to don a parachute. Although badly wounded, Vance took over the controls and crash-landed on the water, but as the plane wallowed to a stop, it exploded. Vance searched unsuccessfully for the wounded man, then floated for almost an hour until a rescue boat arrived. After receiving treatment in England, he boarded a Douglas C-54 transport for the flight to the United States, where he was to receive further medical care. Somewhere over the Atlantic, the plane vanished; no trace was ever found of the aircraft or those on board. Vance joined Snuffy Smith on the roll of men whose heroism merited the Medal of Honor.

The makeup of the bomber crews changed as the war progressed, with more wartime officers moving into positions of command. Few of the enlisted men—whether crew members, mechanics or administrators—had served in the prewar Air Corps. Indeed, by the time the war ended many a sergeant had originally volunteered for flight training only to be declared surplus to the anticipated needs of the service and retrained in some enlisted specialty. Whatever their backgrounds, the vast majority of officers and men overcame their fears, risking death to carry the war into Germany.

Bomber crew is interrogated on return to base

4. Launching the Offensive

With both their British allies and their American superiors looking over their shoulders, Spaatz and Eaker tried to get their bombers into the fight as quickly as possible. Construction of airfields moved smoothly ahead, as the British work crews poured concrete and erected buildings. Aviation engineers assigned to the Eighth Air Force began arriving in January 1942 to perform routine base maintenance and to convert the austere British accommodations to the more comfortable American standard.

Although its leaders had staked their reputations on the big bombers, the Eighth Air Force was a balanced organization with fighters, light bombers and attack planes in addition to the B-17s and B-24s. Indeed, the first combat unit to arrive was the 15th Bombardment Squadron, which arrived in May 1942 and immediately began training in twin-engine Douglas Bostons, the equivalent of the American A-20C attack bomber, borrowed from the Royal Air Force. Next came the 31st Pursuit Group, which disembarked in June. Since this organization, too, had left its own aircraft in the United States, it borrowed Spitfires from the British.

Major J. R. Hawkins, who commanded the 31st Pursuit Group, supervised the transition from the Bell P-39 to the faster, more maneuverable Spitfire. Besides providing the aircraft, the RAF taught the Americans how to fly them in combat. Hawkins's airmen had to learn to maintain formation at treetop height, hugging the earth so that hills and other natural obstacles would reflect German radar beams. Keeping formation, navigating with the aid of unfamiliar checkpoints and carefully adjusting fuel consumption to coax the maximum range out of the planes were techniques that proved as difficult to master as they were essential in combat.

Once the Americans had learned these basic lessons, leaders of the group's squadrons, flights and even two-plane elements temporarily joined British units to fly as wingmen on fighter sweeps over occupied Europe. In mid-August the 31st Pursuit became operational, and it was transferred to the south of England to begin flying under British control, with each of the three American squadrons serving with a different wing of RAF No. 11 Group. Even as other U.S. fighter units were beginning to arrive in Britain, the 31st Pursuit became the first operational American fighter group. Other Americans, however, already were flying Spitfires in combat. They were the volunteer members of the three American Eagle Squadrons, which transferred from the RAF to the U.S. Army Air Forces during September 1942.

Like the first fighter pilots to arrive in England, the members of Major J. L. Griffith's 15th Bombardment Squadron were training under British airmen, who all but adopted their American cousins. The RAF veterans could provide more intensive instruction to this organization than was possible with the larger fighter group. As a result, Griffith's squadron responded so quickly that it received the honor of flying the first American mission against German-held Europe. The ideal date for such an attack was Independence Day, 4 July 1942.

The symbolic importance of this strike was so great that the newly appointed theater commander, Lieutenant General Dwight D. Eisenhower, joined Eaker in visiting Swanton Morley, where the 15th Bombardment Squadron was based, and talking with the Americans who would strike this first blow. The operation order called for the six crews of the Eighth Air Force squadron to join six British crews in a low-altitude daylight attack against four airdromes in Holland.

Luckily, the fact that the raid took place was more important than its results, for the dozen Bostons accomplished very little. Only two of the six American planes hit their assigned targets; the others either got lost or encountered such heavy antiaircraft fire that they could not attack. Indeed, flak downed two planes and badly damaged another. The British meanwhile lost one Boston, damaged by antiaircraft fire and finished off by the only enemy fighter that intercepted the raiders. The greater number of American losses did not, however, result solely from inexperience, for Griffith's men encountered savage antiaircraft fire, especially at two of the airfields, De Kooy and Haamstede.

The gunners defending De Kooy shot away the starboard propeller on the Boston flown by Captain Charles C. Kegelman. His plane dipped sharply, striking the ground and rebounding into the air. As he struggled to climb away from the target, gunners in a nearby flak tower trained their weapons on him, but he reacted coolly, flying directly at the structure and silencing the enemy fire with the machine guns in the jowls of his Boston. Kegelman brought the attack bomber safely home and received the Distinguished Service Cross for his skill and heroism.

Although the 4 July attack was scarcely a victory, it did serve to announce the launching of an American air offensive from the British Isles. The Eighth Air Force, in Captain Kegelman, had its first hero. The real test, however, would not come until the Flying Fortresses and Liberators tried to carry the war to Germany.

In the meantime, the buildup continued, the American bomber force gradually increasing in both numbers and proficiency. Even though Arnold, Spaatz and Eaker were determined to test their theory of daylight strategic bombing, and the British curious just how long the experiment would last, the first complete American heavy bomber group did not reach the United Kingdom until 27 July. Instead of needing a brief familiarization, as the American generals had hoped, this organization, the 97th Bombardment Group, proved to be ill prepared for combat. Part of the problem stemmed from unfamiliar surroundings and rapidly changing weather, but basic failings required intensive retraining.

Dispatched to Britain as soon as it seemed able to fly the Atlantic ferry route, the 97th Bombardment Group arrived with very little experience in high-altitude formation flying. Few radio operators could send or receive in Morse code, and the gunners had seldom fired at towed aerial targets. Many hours of flying had to be crammed into a few short

Flak ignites a twin-engine Douglas A-20

Major General Carl Spaatz (r.), Eighth
Air Force commander

weeks before these men would be able to conduct high-altitude precision bombing, relying mainly on their own guns for survival.

To whip the group into shape, Eaker called upon Colonel Frank A. Armstrong, who had accompanied him to England to set up the Eighth Air Force. By the middle of August, Armstrong had declared two dozen crews ready for combat, each of them a 10-man team whose members had breathed oxygen through the standard mask, endured the cold and learned to clear jammed guns without suffering frostbite. Guns often had to be cleared, for with the lubricants then in use the .50-caliber weapon performed sluggishly and often failed. Another weakness noted by the group was the lack of a power-operated turret in the nose, something that Boeing would correct in later models of the Flying Fortress.

On 17 August, as General Spaatz looked on, 12 B-17Es took off from Grafton Underwood, formed into two six-plane flights, and headed toward the Sotteville railroad marshaling yard at Rouen in northern France. Flying in the lead bomber of the second flight was General Eaker, determined to see for himself how Armstrong's group performed. Escorted by two waves of Spitfires, one relieving the other, the Flying Fortresses dropped almost 37,000 pounds of bombs from about 23,000 feet, depositing roughly half the explosives in the target complex, which included repair shops and cargo depots, along with the maze of rails that accommodated some 2,000 freight cars. Although roadbed proved easy to repair, the damage to buildings almost certainly inconvenienced the enemy. Obviously, far larger numbers of American bombers would have to attack targets of greater importance if the Germans were really to suffer under daylight attack.

Eaker and Spaatz found this first daylight heavy bomber strike especially encouraging. Flak had been light and just three Messerschmitt Me 109s had appeared; they had made ineffectual passes at the formation. The only injuries suffered by American crewmen were cuts from flying glass when a pigeon crashed through the plexiglas nose of one of the bombers.

Throughout the remainder of 1942 the Eighth Air Force bombed targets in German-occupied Europe, always operating with fighter escort. Since German submarines threatened the Atlantic lifeline, B-17s and B-24s bombed the submarine pens along the French coast. Strikes of this sort were futile, though Allied intelligence officers did not yet realize it, for the massive slabs of steel-reinforced concrete protecting the U-boat berths were impervious to any available bomb. Usually, how-

The Sotteville railroad yard
(shown in a 1943 raid)

ever, the targets were more suitable; for example, the industrial plants at Lille, France, bombed on 9 October.

But attacking Lille, whatever the damage inflicted, was not battering Germany. The Messerschmitt and Focke-Wulf factories remained unscathed, even though American gunners claimed an impressive number of fighters destroyed over western Europe. The British, possibly benefiting from Ultra, the intelligence operation that enabled them to break German codes, correctly discounted the American claims.

Prime Minister Churchill, intent upon invading North Africa, was losing patience with the Eighth Air Force. "The claims of the Fortresses are probably exaggerated three-fold," he grumbled, and, he added, "not a bomb has been dropped on Germany." As a result, he favored letting Royal Air Force Bomber Command pound Germany by night, while Eaker's B-17s and B-24s patrolled the seas to safeguard the invasion convoys bound for the African coast.

When Spaatz departed for a command in North Africa, Eaker took over the Eighth Air Force. During December 1942, however, bad

P-47 Thunderbolts were early bomber escorts

weather limited the number of bombing days to only three. Each of these times, the bombers hit a target in France: the Rouen railyards once again; Romilly, which lay southeast of Paris; and the impregnable submarine pens at Lorient. These raids could scarcely persuade Churchill that the daylight bombers were pulling their weight.

In January 1943 at Casablanca, one of the first conquests in the successful invasion of North Africa, the Allied military and political leaders met to chart the course of the war. General Arnold, a member of the American delegation, overheard the British Prime Minister ask President Roosevelt about discontinuing the daylight bombing effort. An emergency call went out for Ira Eaker, who got on extremely well with Churchill. Upon reaching Casablanca, the Eighth Air Force commander and Captain James Parton, who had accompanied him from England, hurried to Arnold's villa and set to work on a document entitled "The Case for Day Bombing," the kind of one-page synopsis the Prime Minister preferred.

The paper emphasized the importance of "bombing the devils around the clock," the Eighth Air Force by day and Bomber Command by night. "We can," the Americans suggested, "ignite obscure targets by day which the RAF can bomb that night by the light of our fires." Chosen to present the case for day bombing was Eaker himself, who reported to the British leader's villa on the morning of 20 January.

According to Eaker, Churchill made a magnificent entrance, wearing the uniform of an air commodore in deference to the fact that he was receiving an airman. After the usual pleasantries—the Prime Minister paid tribute to the courage of American aircrews, and Eaker praised Churchill's willingness to hear both sides of any issue—the general handed over the typed page. The phrase that won the battle, as Eaker delighted in recounting, was "bomb the devils around the clock," a goal that fascinated his host. The Eighth Air Force would have an opportunity to participate by day in the kind of unremitting attack that Eaker had described.

As it happened, General Eaker returned to the British Isles just in time for the first American raid against Germany. On 27 January Colonel Frank Armstrong, now in command of the 306th Bombardment Wing, led a strike force to Vegesack, only to find it hidden by cloud. He succeeded, however, in finding Wilhelmshaven, an alternate target. Bombing through broken cloud, the Americans encountered inaccurate flak, and the 100 or so fighters that swarmed about them failed to press their attacks. The daytime aerial campaign against Germany was off to an encouraging start.

The tempo of the daylight offensive increased, with strikes against other German cities like Bremen, Emden, Hamm and Oschersleben, where Flight Officer Morgan earned his Medal of Honor. The B-17s and B-24s also attacked targets in the occupied countries, sometimes with unexpected results, as happened at Brussels on 28 June 1943. During an attack on an airfield, the bomb release on one of the B-17s malfunctioned, dumping two and one-half tons of explosive on the homes nearby. A horrified young bombardier was greatly relieved to learn that, according to reports from the underground, German troops had commandeered these houses, so that the misdirected bombs had caused 1,000 enemy casualties.

Among the biggest disappointments of the war thus far was the auxiliary fuel tank designed for the Republic P-47 fighter. The first of these planes had reached England in January 1943, but without a satisfactory tank they could fly little farther than the short-legged Spitfires. Eaker wanted the P-47s to escort his formations deep into Germany, but the jug-shaped fighters had to turn back near the border.

To furnish protection beyond the Aachen area, Major Robert Reed proposed hanging as many guns as possible on a B-17, thus making it a flying porcupine that would hover on the fringes of the bomber formations, beating off German interceptors so the bomb-laden Fortresses or Liberators could get through. Major Robert B. Keck took command of 13 of these converted bombers, called YB-40s, which mounted 14 machine guns, eight of them in four power turrets. But the weight of additional armor, guns and ammunition more than made up for the missing bombs and bombsight, making the YB-40 too slow to be of value.

Despite the failure of Reed's converted bomber and the problems with the P-47, prospects seemed to be improving for Eaker's command. The number of bombers and trained crews steadily increased, as the Eighth Air Force recovered from the diversion of men and equipment to North Africa. This theater, however, again beckoned during the summer of 1943, when three B-24 groups deployed to Libya for an attack upon the oil refineries at Ploesti, Rumania. Chosen for the mission were the 93d, commanded by Colonel Ted Timberlake, Leon Johnson's 44th and another group, the 389th, assigned to Eaker but not yet committed to combat. These units joined two Liberator groups already in the theater to cross the Mediterranean Sea and make a low-altitude attack on this important target.

B-24 hits Ploesti at almost smokestack level

Liberators leave Ploesti oil tanks in flames

Like so many of the early operations, the 1 August 1943 raid on Ploesti was more remarkable for heroism—five men won the Medal of Honor—than for results. Even though the crews had practiced on a mock-up of the refinery complex built in the Libyan desert, the confusing terrain along the approach route could not be duplicated. Part of the force took a wrong turn and bombed someone else's target, setting fires that sent clouds of dense smoke into the air and increased the confusion. Despite the raging flames little permanent damage was done, and American losses were disheartening, 54 of 177 planes lost and 532 of 1,726 crewmen killed, captured or interned after crash-landing in neutral Turkey.

Four of the day's Medal of Honor winners were members of the groups borrowed from the Eighth Air Force. Leon Johnson received his award for leading the 44th Bombardment Group through smoke and bursting flak to bomb its assigned target. Two members of the 93d Group were awarded posthumous medals, Colonel Addison Baker and Major John Jerstad, seated side by side at the controls of a B-24 called *Hell's Wench*. When antiaircraft fire tore into their plane three miles short of its objective, they had to jettison their bombs to stay aloft but pooled their strength, wrestling the sluggish controls to lead the group to the refinery. Once the Liberators behind them had seen the target, Baker and Jerstad put the bomber in a climb so the crew could bail out, but the fuselage was already enveloped in flame, and no one escaped. A posthumous award also honored First Lieutenant Lloyd D. Hughes of the 389th Bombardment Group, who held his plane on course until fuel streaming from the tanks was ignited by flame from burning refinery buildings.

On 17 August the Eighth Air Force bombardment groups that had remained in England launched the most ambitious effort of the war. Colonel Curtis LeMay led 147 B-17s to bomb the Messerschmitt plant at Regensburg, Germany, then continued on to airfields near Bône, Tunisia, from which his planes were to launch another strike en route back to England. At the same time 230 Flying Fortresses, led by Brigadier General Robert B. Williams, tried to take advantage of the distraction caused by LeMay's force to bomb the ball-bearing factories at Schweinfurt, also deep inside Germany, and return to the British Isles. Because every implement of war from tanks to submarines required these precisely machined bearings, the Schweinfurt manufacturing complex offered a critical target.

The plan, unfortunately, went awry from the outset. LeMay got his men into the air despite a persisting fog, but the weather kept Williams's crews on the ground. Instead of taking off nine minutes after the Regensburg contingent, the Flying Fortresses bound for Schweinfurt trailed the other force by more than three hours. Each formation therefore had to fight its own separate battle, LeMay's in the morning and Williams's in the afternoon.

Until it reached the vicinity of Aachen, the Regensburg strike force had the protection of a formation of Republic P-47s, but these Thunderbolts had reached the limit of their endurance about the time the first German fighters, Focke-Wulf FW 190s, appeared. The bombers were on their own, handicapped by a sprawling formation that lacked the cohesion necessary for mutual self-defense. Fifteen miles separated the lead bomber, which carried Colonel LeMay, from Tail-end Charlie, the low man at the rear of the entire formation. Taking advantage of the gaps that had opened among the units, the interceptors concentrated upon the 100th Bombardment Group, which brought up the rear.

Among the first of the day's victims was the Tail-end Charlie among LeMay's 147 bombers, a B-17 flown by Captain Robert Knox. A Messerschmitt Me 109, a type manufactured at the very plant Knox was supposed to bomb, bored in head-on, taking a succession of hits from American guns but coming so close that navigator Ernest Warsaw could see the face of the dying German before the fighter stalled and fell into a spin. Before death silenced the interceptor's guns, their fire had knocked out one of the bomber's engines, forcing Knox to reverse course and head for England.

Scarcely had the Flying Fortress come to the heading that Warsaw wanted, when a dozen or more German fighters approached from the rear. The navigator called the pilot and copilot over the interphone but got no reply, as the bomber flew serenely on. Meanwhile, the enemy planes came gradually within range of the weapons on board the B-17. The gunners abruptly opened fire, damaging or shooting down several of the enemy, but the surviving fighters shot the B-17 to pieces. Although Warsaw tried repeatedly to contact Knox or his copilot, there was no response. Both officers, the navigator decided, were dead at the controls, with the automatic pilot guiding the plane.

Warsaw was among those who parachuted safely from the doomed bomber, but his landing knocked him out. When he regained consciousness, he was surrounded by Gestapo men. Since he was a Jew, with an

Formation of Fortresses wheels over Schweinfurt

Bomber commanders: General Hansell (1.), Colonel LeMay

appropriate mark on his dog tags to indicate religious affiliation, his prospects for survival seemed dim. Luckily he managed to throw away the metal identification disc as his captors were driving him to a prison camp.

The death struggle of this bomber may have had unfortunate consequences for the 100th Bombardment Group. As the German fighters had been making their leisurely approach, Warsaw had noticed that the B-17's wheels were down, probably the result of damage to the hydraulic system. At that stage of the war, lowering the landing gear during combat signaled surrender, which explained why the enemy had closed in so carelessly. Because a Flying Fortress bearing the markings of this group had suddenly opened fire after apparently surrendering, German pilots may have concentrated on shooting down aircraft with the organization's symbols, helping the group acquire the nickname Bloody Hundredth.

LeMay led the surviving bombers to Regensburg, bombed the Messerschmitt plant and continued on to Africa. Lost that day were 24 bombers and 240 men killed or captured. Nor had LeMay's troubles ended when the planes, dozens of them severely damaged and with additional dead or wounded on board, landed at Bône and Telergma airfields. The promised repair facilities had not materialized, and LeMay's force, instead of bombing another target while en route back to En-

gland, had taken itself out of the war until it could undergo extensive repairs at the well-equipped East Anglia airfields.

Meanwhile, Williams and his 230 bombers fought their way to Schweinfurt and back, leaving a trail of blossoming parachutes—yellow German and white American—and burning aircraft in their wake. One of the white chutes belonged to Sergeant Delmar Kaech, a radioman who also operated the machine gun in his compartment. When the B-17 in which he was flying began its final plunge, smoke already filled the airplane, and he could barely find his parachute, though it was hanging nearby. Forced to jump before he had the straps securely fastened, the sergeant almost lost the chute when its canopy snapped open, but despite the pain of a slipped disc in his spine, the result of the parachute's opening shock, he clung to the harness and lived.

The bomber from which Kaech jumped, *Eagle's Wrath*, was one of the 36 bombers shot down during the Schweinfurt mission. The bombing had been accurate, fires had ruined sensitive machinery and ball-bearing production declined by 38 percent. Albert Speer, Adolf Hitler's economic chief, drew upon emergency stockpiles until the battered factories began recovering. This brilliant organizer realized, however, that prompt follow-up attacks, coupled with raids on other ball-bearing plants, could cripple the German war effort.

The feared second attack did not come for two months, even though Bomber Command went into action the very night of the first Schweinfurt attack. The British target was Peenemünde, an island off the Baltic coast, rather than the ball-bearing industry.

This Royal Air Force raid on Peenemünde resulted from a combination of deductions, including evidence from the Ultra code-breaking operation. Aerial photographs confirmed that new types of weapons— the V-1 and the V-2—were undergoing evaluation at the research center located on the island. The bombing of Peenemünde delayed the introduction of these vengeance weapons, but the night bombers might have inflicted irreparable damage at Schweinfurt had they attacked there.

Actually, systematic attacks upon key industrial plants, such as the ball-bearing factories, had no place in the current plans of "Bomber" Harris, chief of Bomber Command. He doubted the value of what he termed "panacea targets" and preferred to attack entire cities, "dehousing" German workers and thus crippling production by creating masses of sullen refugees and destroying the will to produce.

Despite the special mission against Peenemünde, Harris pursued these goals, using the latest navigation aids and target markers to fight the Battle of Hamburg, lasting from late July until mid-November 1943. During this period, Bomber Command launched 33 powerful attacks against German cities, devastating Hamburg with four raids by 500 to 750 planes. In addition, Harris's night bombers raided Berlin, Hanover, Kassel, Mannheim and other cities, battering some of them with explosives tonnages that rivaled the amounts dumped on Hamburg.

While Bomber Command pounded an increasing number of German cities, the Eighth Air Force bound up the wounds it had incurred during the Schweinfurt and Regensburg strikes. Besides losing 60 aircraft shot down, Eaker's bomber force reported that another 87 had either crash-landed or sustained damage that sent them to the salvage yard. Moreover, the surviving crews were exhausted mentally and physically, so that 10 days passed before the general could launch another strike, this one an attack against concrete bunkers being built near Calais to launch buzz bombs that had been tested at Peenemünde.

On 6 September, after three other attacks against objectives in France, 388 bombers headed for Stuttgart, but cloud hid the target. Although 262 of the raiders succeeded in bombing other targets through gaps in the clouds, the results were not worth the effort expended, especially since 45 bombers and 450 men failed to return that day.

From Washington, General Arnold kept prodding Eaker to launch more bombers against Germany, even though bad weather persisted. Flying Fortresses did hit Emden twice, bombing through cloud cover with the aid of a radar set developed by the British. But lurking in the consciousness of all of Eaker's men was the knowledge that the Eighth Air Force would someday have to return to Schweinfurt. This formless dread took concrete shape on 14 October, when briefing officers all over England uncovered their maps to reveal that the day's target would be the familiar ball-bearing factories.

For veteran crewmen, word that they were bound for Schweinfurt brought back memories of the earlier battle; for newcomers, the announcement aroused feelings of anxiety, since all of them had heard stories of the August raid. Some of the old-timers put on their good wool uniforms instead of the shapeless fatigues usually worn beneath their flight suits; they wanted to look their best on what might be their last mission.

The Bloody Hundredth did not fly as a unit in the second Schweinfurt raid. From an authorized 48 bombers, the number of aircraft had declined through combat losses, accidents and hard usage until the

Smoke arises from ball bearing plants
hit on 14 October 1943

group had been able to launch only 15 Flying Fortresses against Bremen on 8 October, losing eight of them. On the 10th of the month, 13 B-17s had taken off for Münster, but only one had returned. The eight bombers available for action on the 14th flew with other organizations.

A total of 377 bombers formed up over England late that October morning, but 36 Liberators became lost en route to the assembly point. Their absence forced Brigadier General Fred Anderson, Eaker's bomber commander, to send instructions from his High Wycombe command post for the other 24 B-24s to bomb an alternate target. Two dozen of these aircraft could not generate enough defensive firepower for the long flight to Schweinfurt. Mechanical failure caused two dozen B-17s to turn back, so that when German fighters made their first attacks, fewer than 300 bombers massed their fire against them.

This day's battle proved as vicious as the 17 August fighting had been. Fortresses began plummeting to earth minutes after the P-47s had to turn back. Parachutes again blossomed in the skies of Germany, but too many times there were no chutes when one of the bombers went down. One crewman owed his life to his parachute, but not for the usual reason; a 20-mm shell exploded in the packed chute lying near him, the folded silk canopy miraculously absorbing the concussion and deadly fragments.

To the sweating pilots, struggling to keep the formations from disintegrating as more and more bombers plunged earthward, it seemed for a time that the bombers would not get through, but the survivors persevered. If anything, the bombing on 14 October did more damage than the earlier raid had inflicted. Fire erupted in the tanks containing oil used to bathe the bearings during the machining process, and the resulting heat ruined delicate milling equipment.

The Flying Fortresses now had to fight their way back to England. First Lieutenant Edward Downs, a copilot, took over when the pilot sitting next to him was killed. Even though his own arm was severely gashed, Downs refused morphine, since the safety of the plane depended upon his remaining conscious. He had the navigator, Lieutenant Miles McFann, sit in the pilot's seat and told him how to keep the plane flying straight and level on its three functioning engines.

An overcast shrouded the English countryside when McFann approached the nearest airfield, but an alert RAF base commander heard the bomber and sent two Spitfires aloft to lead it down through the clouds. While McFann handled the throttles, Downs manipulated the

47

Despite this kind of damage, the Germans salvaged machinery

control yoke and rudder, easing the craft through the murk until the field was in sight, then bringing the plane in for a rough but safe landing.

The second attack on Schweinfurt cost the Eighth Air Force 60 bombers shot down. Once again Albert Speer braced himself for additional raids against the ball-bearing industry, but none came. As a result, he had time to carry out plans, drawn up after the August strike, for the dispersal of ball-bearing production. He also supervised both repair of bomb damage at Schweinfurt and the development of ceramic bearings that could, for some uses, replace the steel type.

The two raids on Schweinfurt had demonstrated the accuracy and effectiveness of daylight precision bombing. The price of success had been too high, however, for the Eighth Air Force could not survive as a fighting force if it lost 15 percent or more of the planes and crews dispatched into Germany. Without an escort fighter to reduce these losses, the Army Air Forces could not sustain its share of the around-the-clock bomber offensive that Eaker had described for Winston Churchill at Casablanca.

The self-defending bomber formation had been unable to defeat Germany's fighter force. The Luftwaffe had created a defensive array more formidable than Air Corps theoreticians had dreamed possible when the prototype Flying Fortress took to the air. Until a suitable escort fighter appeared, enemy airmen could keep the American bombers under unremitting attack for as long as the strike force remained over German soil.

5. The Defenses of Germany

The first sign of a daylight raid was an increase in the radio traffic monitored by German listening posts in western Europe. As the Liberators or Flying Fortresses gained altitude and headed toward their target, they came under radar surveillance. Since the bomber formations had to have good weather to use the Norden sight, the huge armadas were visible from the ground; indeed, they frequently left vapor trails as they cruised through the substratosphere. To counter the daylight threat, the Luftwaffe deployed its fighter squadrons in the occupied countries so that they could engage the strike force long before it reached German soil. Ideally, the defenders would destroy or scatter the bombers en route to their objective, but in practice this aim was not achieved. Weather, however, occasionally succeeded where the human defenders failed, forcing the raiders to turn back or attack a secondary target.

Reports concerning the size and course of the approaching formation went to controllers on the ground, who committed fighters that were within range of the Americans. Once aloft, the pilots responded to instruction radioed either from the ground or from veteran pilots who served as airborne coordinators. Standard tactics called for the interceptors to fight in two-man cells—*Rotten*—each made up of a leader and his wingman, or four-man flights, *Schwärme*, each consisting of two cells, with the leader of one doubling as flight leader. Until the bombers acquired power-operated nose turrets, German pilots preferred to attack head-on. The reason for this choice was obvious. In every Luftwaffe dayroom hung a chart depicting a B-17E in flight and showing the cone of fire from every gun position. To engage a fighter attacking from 12 o'clock, directly ahead of the bomber, these Fortresses and also the early-model Liberators had to rely primarily on hand-operated machine guns.

Even after detailed charts and exhaustive briefings, the first sight of a bomber formation was awe-inspiring. The young fighter pilot remembered those cones cross-hatched on the chart and wondered how he could possibly penetrate the wall of fire all around these four-engine monsters. While other flights feinted toward the Americans, the new man stayed with his cell and flight leaders, following them to a point well in front of the massed bombers, then knifing to the attack. The closing speed of fighter and bomber exceeded 500 miles per hour, giving the fighter pilot about two seconds to get the small frontal silhouette in his sights and fire, while the nose guns and possibly the dorsal turret were blazing away at him. If he broke off the attack too soon or rolled away in an unexpected direction, he risked collision with his cell leader or another plane in the *Schwarm*. If he waited too long before breaking off his assault, he might collide with his intended victim or end up flying the length of the formation, coming under fire from dozens of guns as he swept past.

One pass did not mean the end of the day's fighting for German pilots. After exhausting their ammunition, they landed, rearmed and refueled to attack again. As a result, the Americans could expect repeated fighter passes from the time their own escort of P-47s or Spitfires had to leave them until it met them as they came back from the day's target. Occasionally a German airman might be shot down in the morning and parachute safely, and then get back into action that afternoon, when the bombers were returning to England. At the time, German doctrine dictated that aviators parachute immediately if their fighters sustained severe damage, for it was regarded as easier to replace the plane than to train another pilot to take the place of one killed unnecessarily in a crash landing.

Not everyone followed these orders. The twin-engine Messerschmitt Me 110 could absorb heavy punishment, and one crew managed to fly two missions in a single day even though the first burst of American gunfire had cracked the main wing spar. With the single-seat Me 109, however, only a fool or a superb aviator ignored serious damage. If this fighter nosed over out of control, the speed increased so rapidly that within seconds the pilot could not force his way out of the cockpit.

The Luftwaffe hurled both single-engine and twin-engine fighters against the daylight formations. Less dangerous were the twin-engine types, usually Me 110s or Me 210s, a newer product of the same firm. Designed by Willy Messerschmitt as a long-range escort fighter, the Me 110 was heavily armed, mounting a pair of forward-firing 20-mm cannon and as many as four light machine guns, plus another 7.9-mm machine gun on a swivel mount at the rear of the glass-enclosed cockpit. Pitted against Hurricanes and Spitfires in the Battle of Britain, the early models lacked the speed and maneuverability to protect themselves, let alone the bombers they were escorting.

The Me 110 became an adequate night fighter, and it enjoyed some success against daylight formations. Occasionally an Me 110 or Me 210 might conceal itself in a vapor trail, approach within range of a bomber and open fire before the tail gunner spotted it. The usual role assigned to these aircraft during the air battles of 1943 was to disrupt the bomber formation with rockets or bombs, for even the B-17 could not fight off a swarm of attackers once it had left the mutual protection of the combat box.

Willy Messerschmitt's Me 109 had gone through dozens of modifications since its first flight in 1935. Early models had seen combat in the Spanish Civil War and the conquest of Poland. Now, in the summer of 1943, the Me 109G proved deadly in combat, though tricky to fly. This variant mounted a pair of 20-mm cannon plus machine guns—adequate firepower for the job at hand—but the Daimler-Benz liquid-cooled engine could deliver up to 1,800 horsepower, more power than the basic design could accommodate. Pilots had to be especially careful of speed during dives, and landings remained a challenge. The bigger engine increased the landing speed for a type of aircraft that had always tended to ground loop because of its narrow landing-gear track. In the hands of a skilled pilot, however, these new Messerschmitts remained among the most formidable of World War II fighters.

The other single-engine interceptor that attacked daylight formations during 1943 was the Focke-Wulf FW 190, designed by Kurt Tank. When it first appeared early in 1941, the plane had outperformed the Spitfire V. Not until the pilot of an FW 190A became lost and landed on the wrong side of the English Channel did British engineers discover what a splendid aircraft Tank had produced. Spitfire pilots already knew that these early FW 190s were faster, more maneuverable and more rugged than contemporary Royal Air Force fighters. Eaker's airmen encountered various species of the FW 190A during 1943. The basic model was powered by a 1,700-horsepower radial engine that could deliver 2,100 horsepower in an emergency. Standard armament was two 13-mm machine guns, two 20-mm cannon in the wing root and two other 20-mm or 30-mm cannon mounted about halfway to the wing tips.

Because they frequently flew two or three sorties on a single day, German fighter pilots downed incredible numbers of Allied aircraft. Among them, the 10 leading Luftwaffe aces destroyed 2,588 planes. The leader, Erich Hartmann, received credit for 352 aerial victories, the result of 1,425 individual sorties—as many as seven on the same day—that resulted in more than 800 air battles. On one combat sortie in his

The Messerschmitt Me 109—veteran but still valuable in 1943

The Focke-Wulf FW 190—fast, maneuverable, rugged

Me 109, Hartmann shot down five American fighters, though he scored most of his victories over Russian airmen, whom he considered ill-trained in comparison to British or American aviators. Sixteen times Hartmann was himself shot down, sometimes parachuting but frequently crash-landing his fighter in violation of Luftwaffe policy.

Günther Rall, credited with 275 victories, enjoyed his successes in the Russian and Mediterranean areas. His career almost ended when he tried to intercept an Eighth Air Force bomber formation only to be jumped by four escorting fighters. The heavy .50-caliber guns crippled his plane and a bullet severed his left thumb, but he managed to parachute safely. He recovered from this wound, his third of the war, and returned to action.

The claims of these German aces were probably no less accurate than those of Allied airmen. Like the Allies, the Germans insisted upon verification of all claims and mounted gun cameras in some aircraft. Yet the confusion of aerial combat, the amazing ability of an aircraft like the B-17 to absorb punishment without breaking up and the fact that several independent witnesses might report the same aerial victory complicated the task of compiling valid statistics.

Besides interceptors flown by veterans like Rall, the Eighth Air Force had to contend with antiaircraft fire. During daylight the Germans normally used optical devices to track the formation as it approached the batteries defending the target. In bad weather, however, radar data could be fed into the fire-control equipment that provided instructions for the gunners. The early fire-control predictor could not track aircraft unless they flew in a straight line at speeds under 400 miles per hour, but German engineers corrected these failings so that the equipment could follow its prey through a turn even though the actual speed reached 600 miles per hour. If the fire-control device performed to perfection and the gun batteries reacted promptly, the formation would be engaged above a point 10,000 yards from the target. As a result, the Americans would have to fly through bursting flak for three and one-half miles before reaching the bomb release point an estimated 4,000 yards short of the objective.

A variety of antiaircraft weapons defended key targets throughout Germany and the occupied countries. The lightest weapon that normally engaged the high-flying B-17s and B-24s was the versatile 88-mm gun, capable of reaching a plane 35,000 feet away and firing 20 rounds per minute. The barrel heated rapidly, however, and gunners had to pause briefly after every 25 rounds or so and allow it to cool. A 105-mm weapon fired a heavier shell than the 88-mm type but could not reach beyond 31,000 feet and had a slightly slower rate of fire. The heaviest weapon encountered by the Eighth Air Force was the 128-mm gun, usually mounted in pairs on flak towers in Germany's largest cities. These giants could hurl a 57-pound shell to 35,000 feet, but their rate of fire did not exceed 10 rounds per minute, despite the use of a hydraulic loading mechanism.

The urban flak towers differed from those encountered by the borrowed Douglas Bostons during the 4 July 1942 attack upon airfields in Holland. The latter towers contained mostly automatic weapons sited to protect the bases. Besides being much larger, comparable in size to office buildings, the flak towers built to defend German cities mounted heavy guns, 88-mm to 128-mm, at all four corners, with lighter weapons to deal with any low-flying raiders.

Proof of the importance that the Luftwaffe placed on antiaircraft defenses was the number of persons assigned to this task. The force was growing in the summer of 1943, but during the following year it would attain a peak strength of about 1,250,000 men and women. Not all of them, however, were engaged in defending German cities, for combat units also received antiaircraft protection.

The nighttime defenses of Germany had undergone revolutionary change since the days when Whitleys wandered about unmolested to drop their leaflets. In the beginning the Luftwaffe had relied on searchlights deployed around key cities to illuminate bombers for Me 109s patrolling in the darkness. All this had begun changing when Josef Kammhuber assumed responsibility for defending Germany against night attack. He left the defense of the immediate target area to flak bat-

Adolf Galland (center), Germany's
General of the Fighter Arm

teries, assisted by the searchlights, fitted out twin-engine night fighters having greater endurance than the Me 109, and employed radar to control these aircraft.

From Schleswig in northwestern Germany to St. Dizier, east of Paris, Kammhuber established a defensive belt consisting of radar-equipped ground control stations and airfields at which night fighters were based. Early warning radars picked up the British formations in time for the defenders to take off. At each ground control station one highly accurate radar tracked the enemy, while another kept watch on the defenders, so that the controllers could coach the fighters into position to intercept.

The nightfighter units generally flew Me 110s, Junkers Ju 88s or Dornier Do 17s. Of these, only the Messerschmitt had been designed as a fighter. The others were converted twin-engine bombers fitted with additional guns. Since the planes did not yet carry airborne radar, the crewmen depended upon their eyesight. They tried to approach the bomber stream from below in order to remain hidden against the darkened earth as they sought to silhouette the bomber against the lighter sky.

If one of his crew members reported the approaching fighter, the bomber pilot immediately began corkscrewing to spoil the German's aim. These tactics could prove effective, for even the huge British Lancaster was difficult to hit in the dark, and the fighter had to contend with possible fire from the four .303 guns in the bomber's rear turret and with prop wash from the intended victim's four engines. Flying into the wake of one of the bombers was like hitting an invisible wall.

Many times the British crew did not see the enemy. A total of 97 night bombers fell victim to Lieutenant Colonel Helmut Lent before his death in October 1944 from injuries suffered in a flying accident. The leading night ace, however, was Major Heinz-Wolfgang Schnaufer, "the Night Ghost of St. Trond," who scored most of his 121 victories in a defensive sector due west of Bonn.

Searchlights and antiaircraft guns defended the target itself. The lights themselves were capable of blinding a crew, besides picking out the aircraft for the gunners below. At times, British crews reported seeing a shell, which they called scarecrow, that resembled an exploding bomber when it burst. In fact, no shell existed; what the airmen saw were bombers actually exploding, usually shot down by unseen night fighters.

As the defenses of Germany grew more difficult to penetrate, by day or night, the Americans and their British allies tried a number of hasty solutions, none very successful. Victory in daylight would await the coming of a genuine escort fighter, not a YB-40 bristling with guns. Nor could Bomber Command defeat Kammhuber's night fighters by trying to flood the defensive sectors with more bombers than radar could handle. Some type of jamming device was essential to blind the Luftwaffe controllers.

Bombs fall from a formation above
the B-17 shown

6. Protecting the Bombers

In order to carry out the Anglo-American Combined Bomber Offensive approved at Casablanca, the American daylight bombers needed an escort fighter to protect attacks against German industry. The British night raiders had to devise an array of electronic devices that would enable them to find German cities in the darkness and, on their reaching these targets, would frustrate the radar-controlled defenses deployed by General der Flieger Josef Kammhuber. The Allied bomber force, in short, had to be protected against fighters that swarmed by day around the American formations or prowled the night sky in search of the British bomber stream.

When Eaker's bombers had first arrived in England, two types of fighters then in mass production seemed able to protect them. The more formidable of the pair was the Republic P-47 Thunderbolt, designed by Alexander Kartveli. As it took shape on his drawing board, the Thunderbolt became the heaviest and most powerful high-altitude fighter of its day. To ensure that the plane could fight in the substratosphere, Kartveli and his associates built the craft around a turbosupercharger buried in the fuselage behind the cockpit but capable of forcing air into the 2,000-horsepower radial engine. This power plant propelled the six-ton fighter through the air at speeds in excess of 400 miles per hour. The P-47 mounted eight .50-caliber guns, located in the elliptical wings so as to fire outside the arc of the four-bladed propeller.

Although official press releases referred to the fighter as the Thunderbolt, the men who flew it usually called it the Jug. Some say that this nickname was short for juggernaut, but most likely the aircraft acquired the alias because it looked like a jug—the oval surface of the Pratt and Whitney radial engine serving as base and the vertical stabilizer as handle. The first of the type to see action in Europe were B models, followed in the summer of 1943 by the first P-47Ds. Both were razorback types, so called because of the metal fairing that extended after from the cockpit to the base of the vertical stabilizer.

These early Thunderbolts demonstrated ruggedness and devastating firepower but were cursed by a lack of range. Once a satisfactory auxiliary fuel tank was added, the range increased from 550 to 1,250 miles, provided that the pilot kept close watch on his speed and fuel consumption. Unfortunately, the new tanks appeared too late to benefit the bombers dispatched to Schweinfurt during the summer and fall of 1943. By the end of the war the latest version, the P-47N, boasted a cruising range of 2,350 miles, reflecting additional internal fuel cells, plus larger disposable tanks.

Except for their short range, the early razorback P-47s proved deadly in aerial combat. Colonel Hubert Zemke, in command of the 56th Fighter Group, nicknamed the "Wolfpack," worked out tactics that emphasized the best features of his aircraft. The rugged Thunderbolt could outdive most other types and recover without coming apart. Indeed, an enthusiastic test pilot, thanks to inaccurate instruments on his control panel, reported that he had exceeded the speed of sound in a power dive with one of the first P-47s. Zemke emphasized diving speed and firepower to compensate for the Jug's sluggish rate of climb. He tried always to engage the enemy by diving to the attack, getting off a burst from the eight guns that could shred an Me 109, then rolling into a dive whenever the more maneuverable German fighters gained the advantage. Apparently Zemke knew his airplane, for the Wolfpack, flying P-47Cs, Ds and Ms, claimed a total of 575 aerial victories during the war.

The second fighter available for escort duty early in the war was the Lockheed P-38 Lightning. A team of designers headed by H. L. Hibbard and including Kelly Johnson turned out a radical-looking, twin-engine fighter powered by supercharged Allison liquid-cooled engines. To accommodate the superchargers, the designers placed the engines in booms that extended rearward from the wing and supported the tail surfaces. The pilot sat in a pod, which jutted forward from the wing and contained the standard armament of one 20-mm cannon and four .50-caliber machine guns. The plane featured a tricycle landing gear and propellers that rotated in opposite directions to avoid torque that might have reduced maneuverability. During 1942 and early 1943, P-38F and G fighters arrived in England, but despite their greater range, the Lightnings were less satisfactory than the P-47s.

The RAF had already formed a low opinion of the P-38 on the basis of two specially built models tested in the United Kingdom in the spring of 1942. The British Air Purchasing Commission had insisted that the superchargers be removed and that both propellers have the same right-hand rotation. Unable to fight at high altitude, and difficult to maneuver down low, these test models proved worthless.

The Army Air Forces, however, usually got excellent results with the P-38, especially against the Japanese. In the Pacific the Lightning's combination of heavy firepower and long range made it a deadly weapon against lighter, though more maneuverable, opponents. The Lockheed fighter also performed creditably against German and Italian fighters in North Africa, but over Europe it failed as a bomber escort. Range, however, was not the problem. England's dampness, and the cold encountered on long missions, brought out unsuspected flaws in carburetors and superchargers. Even the newer Lightnings that arrived after the second Schweinfurt raid suffered from these mechanical problems.

A series of lucky breaks at last provided the Eighth Air Force with an excellent fighter capable of escorting the daylight bomber force to Berlin and beyond. The first of these happy accidents occurred in the spring of 1940, when the British Air Purchasing Commission asked J. H. ("Dutch") Kindelberger, president of North American Aviation, to consider manufacturing Curtiss Hawk 81As, export models of the P-40, for delivery to the United Kingdom. Confident of his own organization, Kindelberger proposed an entirely new airplane, powered like the P-40 by an Allison liquid-cooled engine, and promised to finish a prototype in 120 days.

P-47 was officially the "Thunderbolt," unofficially
the "Jug"

In charge of the team of designers handed this impossible assignment were Edgar Schmued and Raymond Rice. They borrowed a landing gear assembly from the Harvard trainer, incorporating it in an aerodynamically clean, low-wing, single-engine design with an airscoop
beneath the fuselage for radiators located aft of the wing. While
Schmued, Rice and their colleagues worked on the general layout, the
company's aerodynamic department, headed by L. L. Waite, suggested
a new airfoil that promised increased maneuverability and range. Using
data obtained from the experimental laboratories of the National Advi-
sory Committee for Aeronautics at Langley Field, Va., Edward Horkey
adapted this laminar flow wing to the NA-73 experimental fighter. The

first Mustang, minus its Allison engine, rolled from the North American factory three days before the deadline set by the company's president.

Actually, the Allison engine was the only serious weakness in the basic Mustang design. As the RAF soon discovered, the new fighter could outperform almost any other aircraft at low altitude, but above 15,000 feet the Allison, which lacked a supercharger, soon was struggling to breathe. At this point luck again intervened, for the British Air Ministry decided to install a supercharged Rolls-Royce Merlin engine in the Mustang, instead of settling for a similarly equipped Allison. Fitted with Merlins manufactured in the United States by the Packard automobile company, the Mustang became the finest fighter of the war.

Although the earliest Merlin-powered Mustang, the P-51B, mounted only four .50-caliber guns, standard armament soon became six

P-38s were not successful escorts over Europe

of these weapons, located in the wings to fire outside the propeller arc. The D and K models, which were almost identical eventually, replaced the older Bs and Cs in Europe. Besides having a bubble canopy that improved visibility during combat, the later P-51s were slightly faster, though all the Merlin-powered Mustangs exceeded 400 miles per hour, and could cruise 2,000 miles with the assistance of auxiliary fuel tanks, slightly less than the maximum cruising range of the P-51B.

Like any new airplane, the P-51 had its share of teething problems. Speed increased rapidly during dives, so that the incautious pilot might easily bury himself in the earth. And the first American-built Merlins proved balky, fouling sparkplugs and sometimes quitting without warning, problems that solved themselves as the engine manufacturer gained experience. Guns on the early Mustangs tended to jam, a problem that puzzled technicians until they realized that the forces exerted during certain high-speed maneuvers pushed cartridges into the weapons out of cycle. Adjustment of the feed mechanisms solved the problem.

If any one airplane won the daytime war in the skies over Germany, that craft was the P-51 Mustang. Lieutenant Colonel James Howard, in command of the 356th Fighter Squadron, proved on 11 January 1944 just how deadly the P-51B could be in the hands of a skilled pilot. A veteran of the Flying Tigers, with 6⅓ aerial victories against the Japanese, Howard had already demonstrated that he was an exceptional combat pilot.

On this particular day, though assigned to the Ninth Air Force, Howard and his men were covering an Eighth Air Force attack on the Focke-Wulf plant at Oschersleben. After downing a twin-engine Me 110, the squadron commander became isolated from his unit and found himself the only American in position to intercept a force of FW 190s and Me 109s closing on the bomber formation. He dived to the attack, fencing with some two dozen of the enemy for almost 30 minutes. The pilot of an Me 109 gave Howard some difficult moments. With the P-51 on his tail, the German suddenly throttled back, but Howard anticipated this action and reduced power, only to have the Messerschmitt double back, dipping beneath the Mustang. Again Howard kept pace with the enemy, who now entered a series of turns, hoping to cut inside the heavier American fighter and score with his own guns. The former Flying Tiger foiled these tactics by lowering his flaps, slowing abruptly, and firing into the Me 109 as it tried to break away. Although this aircraft may have escaped, Howard shot down a total of three German fighters that day and single-handedly prevented what might have been a devastating attack upon the bombers he was protecting, accomplishments that earned him the Medal of Honor.

The Mustang, in short, proved a truly decisive weapon, but it had come into the hands of the Army Air Forces through a series of accidents. American airmen had placed too much confidence in their flying dreadnaughts, the B-17 and B-24, and ignored the long-range fighter. In his memoir, *Global Mission*, General Arnold conceded that the P-51 should have seen combat "rather sooner" than it did.

While fate handed the Mustang to General Arnold, Bomber Harris and Josef Kammhuber used the products of their electronics experts in the fight to control the night skies. The combatants engaged in a life-and-death chess match in which each tried to neutralize any advantage

B-17 unloads a stick of bombs over Bremen

gained by the other. Early in 1942, for example, the British had introduced Gee, a navigational beam that could direct a plane to within one-half to five miles of the intended target. By the end of August, however, the Germans had learned to jam this equipment. British scientists countered with Oboe, Gee's replacement, which went into action in December.

Whereas Gee stations in England had broadcast signals that appeared on a cathode ray tube in the navigation compartment of the bomber, Oboe ground stations transmitted signals that were augmented and rebroadcast from a pathfinder aircraft. By measuring the time the signals were in transit, a controller in England could determine the location of the aircraft and signal when it should release its incendiary bombs or flares to mark the target. With an experienced pathfinder crew, Oboe could be accurate within a few hundred yards of the desired aiming point. Although the Germans failed to jam Oboe, which also was used by the Eighth Air Force for bombing through haze or cloud, the device proved vulnerable to the Allies' own radar. British scientists then modified the equipment to correct this failing.

Both Gee and Oboe declined in accuracy beyond the Ruhr valley. Some other device would be needed for long-range bombing, and once again the electronics wizards rose to the challenge. As early as 1937, Dr. E. G. Bowen had experimented with airborne radar. Working patiently over the years, this British scientist contributed to the eventual development of H2S, an airborne set with which a trained flier could distinguish between land and water, locate built-up areas and sometimes pick out such landmarks as the bend of a river. Since the image seen on the H2S tube did not, however, correspond to the view portrayed on an aerial chart, interpretation was necessary and human error unavoidable. H2S entered service with Bomber Command in January 1943, and by the end of the year American daylight bombers were using H2X, a radar bombing aid based on this British invention.

Late in October 1943, Bomber Command began using G-H, a navigation and blind-bombing aid that combined the features of Gee and Oboe. The major innovation, in fact, consisted of placing the Oboe transmitter in the aircraft, from which it broadcast to the ground stations; the navigator, rather than a controller in England, measured the time intervals and calculated the plane's position. Since the ground terminals now performed a passive role, intensifying and retransmitting the signal, many bomber formations could use this equipment on the same night without overwhelming the capacity of a single control agency.

The P-51 Mustang—the plane that
solved escort problems

These electronic aids helped Bomber Command pierce the darkness to locate their targets, but somewhere in the night lurked German fighters controlled by the precision radars that Kammhuber had scattered across western Europe. The first radar countermeasure available to Bomber Harris was Window, strips of metal foil fabricated to reflect the signal from the radars that Kammhuber's controllers used to coach night fighters onto the bomber stream. This innovation made its debut in August 1943. The return from Window caused "clutter" on the radar scope, a blizzard of reflections that prevented the controller from isolating the return from an aircraft.

Besides using the various navigation aids, the Eighth Air Force sometimes employed these radar reflectors, called Chaff by the Americans, during the daylight operations. One aerial gunner vividly remembers his introduction to Chaff. He was shown a large bundle filled with strips of foil and told to drop it through the hatch in the floor of the navigator's compartment at a certain time during the mission. Word came over the interphone, and the gunner carried out the order. Unfortunately, no one had told him to open the bundle and scatter the Chaff. The slipstream hurled the heavy container against the belly turret, convincing the gunner that the Fortress had taken a direct hit from flak. Half-stunned, he was already struggling out of the turret before the other crewmen could explain what had happened.

To deal with Window, Kammhuber shifted from his original linear defense to a defense in depth, in which his men picked up British electronic signals, such as pulses from the H2S radar, to locate the bomber stream. A ground controller used this information to coach radar-equipped night fighters into position to intercept. As they had in the past, these twin-engine aircraft, among them the new Dornier Do 217 and Heinkel He 219, tried to approach their victims from behind and

slightly below. To facilitate these tactics, some of them carried *Schräge Musik*—"slanting music," a slang term for jazz—which consisted of two 20-mm cannon aimed upward and slightly to the front. The night fighter flew underneath the bomber and fired into the wing root, which housed a large gasoline tank. Many of the scarecrow shells reported by British airmen actually were exploding Lancasters or other aircraft shot down in this fashion.

To supplement the night fighters, called Tame Boars, were the Wild Boars, day fighters like the Me 109 that congregated at navigation beacons, then tried to search out the bomber stream and attack. The use of these fighters, proposed by Hans-Joachim Herrmann, a young bomber pilot, put additional aircraft into the night air battles, but

Flak and searchlights lace the night sky over Germany

crashes were frequent, as pilots tried to land their short-range fighters in the darkness.

The British at first attempted to exploit the German airborne radar, equipping Mosquito bombers with a set that picked up the enemy signal, but the Luftwaffe promptly introduced a different transmitter. More vulnerable was radio communication between controller and his night fighters. Radio operators on certain bombers tried to jam the frequency used by the Germans, and stations in England joined in, sometimes broadcasting false instructions in idiomatic German.

During 1944 the British employed a variety of electronic trickery to defeat Kammhuber's defenses. While a handful of bombers, scattering Window, created a diversion, the actual bomber stream headed toward Germany, also dispensing radar reflectors when judged necessary. Meanwhile, stations in Britain jammed both early warning radar and radio communication. Once the raiders commenced their penetration of Kammhuber's defenses, airborne jamming equipment, mounted in either British or American planes, kept up the harassment of both radar operators and fighter controllers.

This complex array of electronic countermeasures was essential for the survival of Bomber Command. When the night was clear and the moon bright enough for the Wild Boars to seek out their victims, the Luftwaffe could convert a long-range mission into near disaster. On the night of 30–31 March 1944, for instance, these conditions prevailed, and 95 of the 782 heavy bombers launched to attack Nuremberg fell victim to fighters or antiaircraft fire.

The Allies, however, could occasionally accept these losses, despite the individual tragedy that the numbers represented. Factories in the United States and Britain easily replaced lost aircraft, and the Army Air Forces would soon find that it was training more pilots than it could use. Thanks to the Mustang in daylight and the electronic devices employed at night, numbers and industrial strength seemed likely to prevail, though savage fighting lay ahead.

7. Changes at the Top

In the days immediately following the second Schweinfurt raid, the Merlin-powered Mustang had not yet entered combat, though the first squadron would arrive in mid-November, diverted from North Africa to meet the emergency in Europe. Despite the bombing damage inflicted by the 14 October 1943 mission, an emergency clearly existed, for the Eighth Air Force could not survive repeated losses of this magnitude. In a single day, some 600 airmen had been killed or captured, morale had declined as a result, and confidence in the self-defending bomber formation had vanished. Resumption of the daylight offensive would await the coming of the P-51B, and success would depend upon the accomplishments of this aircraft.

For General Arnold the second Schweinfurt raid had come as a severe jolt. On the very day of the attack he had told Eaker that the evidence reaching Washington seemed to indicate that the German air force was on the verge of defeat. Now the commanding general faced

Eighth Air Force fighter pilots listen intently
to intelligence briefing

the difficult problem of convincing the American public that the results of the raid outweighed the losses.

General Eaker realized his superior's predicament and sought to provide him with information to use in an explanation, at the same time requesting the P-51Bs and the disposable fuel tanks that would enable the Eighth Air Force to return to the attack. Eaker advised Arnold that the bombing had been extremely accurate and had caused severe damage, an accurate description, but he also accepted crew reports that 186 German fighters had gone down in flames. This toll, he suggested, indicated that the fighting on 14 October had represented "the last final struggle of a monster in his death throes." He added, "There is not the slightest doubt but that we now have our teeth in the Hun Air Force's neck." But in fact, the Luftwaffe may have lost no more than 40 fighters during the day's battle.

In interpreting the results of the Schweinfurt raid, Arnold radiated confidence. He described the manufacturing complex as a "heap of twisted girders, smoking ruins, and pulverized machinery" that was "completely useless" to the enemy. "We did it in daylight," he boasted, "and we did it with precision, aiming our explosives with the care and accuracy of a marksman firing a rifle at a bull's-eye." Words like these might reassure the public for the time being, but reassurance was not enough. Eaker would have to get his bombers back in action as quickly as possible.

Almost a week passed, however, before the Flying Fortresses again attacked. On 20 October, escorted by P-47s, the bombers raided Düren in western Germany. Another lull, caused in part by bad weather, ensued. Then, on 3 November, Eaker's bombers raided Wilhelmshaven, using the new airborne radar to attack through an overcast. Since the day's objective was a harbor, the sharp contrast between land and water on the lead bombardier's scope permitted a fair degree of accuracy. Once again fighters, this time P-38s, protected the strike force. Obviously, the Eighth Air Force would have to recuperate from the second Schweinfurt raid much as it had from the first.

While General Arnold fretted about the future of daylight bombing, which rested now on the long-range fighter, the Luftwaffe chief, Hermann Göring, railed at his subordinates. On 14 October, immediately after the bombs had stopped falling on Schweinfurt, he had assured Hitler that the air arm had won a decisive victory, leaving the wreckage of American bombers scattered from Aachen to the target and thence to the exit point at the French border near Metz. Albert Speer had then picked up the telephone and discovered that this raid would reduce by two-thirds the nation's output of ball bearings. Thus discredited, an angry Göring now lashed out at his pilots, ignoring what they had accomplished and accusing them of cowardice.

Since the Ultra intelligence operation could not eavesdrop on the furious Reichsmarschall, neither Arnold nor Eaker knew of his discomfiture. The two American officers did, however, know of the success being claimed for night bombing. Thus far, Bomber Command had never experienced losses at night that approached the numbers, or the percentage of the strike force, that had failed to return from the 14 October daylight attack on Schweinfurt. Indeed, during the 33 major night raids launched against German cities during the Battle of Hamburg, only 4.1 percent of the night bombers had failed to return. Now, while Eaker's Flying Fortresses and Liberators, escorted by fighters, probed the fringes of the Reich, Bomber Harris spoke in terms of a Battle of Berlin. He was confident that, if the Americans joined in, aerial bombardment could reduce the city to rubble. The effort, he warned, would cost the Allies between 400 and 500 bombers, but it would "cost Germany the war."

Eaker was optimistic that his command could contribute to winning the victory that Harris described. With almost 750 heavy bombers now under his control, he could dispatch as many as 500 on a single day, provided that the P-51B lived up to its advance notices. Already the first group of Mustangs had extended operations into western Germany. Although assigned to the Ninth Air Force, these retrained P-39 pilots served under the operational control of the Eighth, with Lieutenant Colonel Donald Blakeslee assuming command. On 11 December two dozen of Blakeslee's P-51Bs escorted an attack on Emden, damaging an Me 110, one of the few German fighters that tried to intercept. The first actual test came five days later, over Bremen, when the group tangled with several twin-engine aircraft. Lieutenant Charles Gumm downed an Me 110, scoring the first confirmed victory of the war by the P-51. But as the Mustangs were en route back to England, a group of P-47s mistook them for Me 109s and almost attacked, before realizing the error.

At this stage of the air war, with the brightest days seeming to lie just ahead, Eaker on 18 December received word from General Arnold that he was being replaced as Eighth Air Force commander. His next assignment would be command of Allied air forces in the Mediterranean, a

Colonel Donald Blakeslee (r.) with ace Don
Gentile

General Jimmy Doolittle (r.) with Generals
Spaatz (1.) and George Patton

job he considered less important than command of the Eighth Air Force. His replacement at High Wycombe would be Lieutenant General Jimmy Doolittle, who as a lieutenant colonel had led the famous morale-raising B-25 raid on Tokyo in April 1942. Returning to England was Carl Spaatz, who had turned the Eighth Air Force over to Eaker roughly a year earlier. Spaatz would take command of the new U.S. Strategic Air Forces in Europe, with authority over both the Mediterranean-based Fifteenth Air Force and Doolittle's Eighth.

Aware that no general whose performance satisfies his superiors suddenly finds himself relieved—or, as in this case, given a less important job with a more impressive title—Eaker protested, reminding Arnold that he came to England with the original Eighth Air Force staff, helped shape the organization and led it through its darkest days. He asked to be left in command, if his services had been "satisfactory to seniors," so that he might help bring the daylight bomber offensive to a successful climax.

Not content with an appeal to Arnold, Eaker asked Eisenhower and Spaatz to intercede on his behalf, but the decision proved irrevocable. The Commanding General, Army Air Forces, expressed his gratitude for all Eaker had done and his sympathy that the change affected him "personally," but he refused to reconsider. All that remained was for Eaker to introduce his successor before stepping aside.

En route to his new command, Eaker paused at Casablanca and was summoned to the same villa where he had spoken with Churchill almost a year before. The Prime Minister, recuperating in North Africa from an illness, realized Eaker's disappointment and chose this moment to deliver what amounted to a gracious pep talk. As Eaker departed, Churchill recalled their earlier meeting, remarking that the air war was proceeding almost exactly as the American had described in his paper.

Impatience with the slow recovery from the second Schweinfurt attack was not the only reason behind Arnold's action. In bringing Spaatz to England as the overall commander of American heavy bomber forces in Europe, the commanding general apparently was looking ahead to that day after the war when he would step aside. He had great confidence in Spaatz, who with this appointment became Arnold's heir-apparent, the officer who, it was hoped, would assume command of an independent air arm when the fighting had ended.

Eaker, of course, might have remained as a subordinate to Spaatz, but Doolittle seemed a better choice for the moment and for the postwar future. The new Eighth Air Force commander enjoyed the confidence of Spaatz and Eisenhower, with whom he had worked in North Africa. Further, he would not be a factor in establishing a command structure for the autonomous postwar air force. Before reentering military service with the coming of World War II, Doolittle had been not only a racing pilot but an executive with Shell Oil, and after the conflict he undoubtedly would return to private industry. The vision of a U.S. Air Force, equal in stature to the Army and Navy and commanded by Spaatz, may well have influenced Arnold's decision to replace Eaker with an equally competent officer whose postwar future was not bound up in military aviation.

British leaders, who from the King on down had admired the tactful Eaker, found Spaatz more difficult to deal with, firm in his opinions and confident of his authority. Since Spaatz enjoyed Arnold's trust, he consulted less frequently with the commanding general and was spared the sort of pressure exerted on Eaker as he restored his command to fighting strength after the Regensburg and Schweinfurt raids of August 1943. Of course, circumstances contributed to this independence and immunity from long-distance criticism; thanks to Spaatz's mighty armada of bombers, escorted by Mustangs and improved Thunderbolts, the bleak days of August or October were unlikely to return.

Doolittle, too, proved a more difficult colleague than Eaker, a result in part of the greater strength of the Eighth Air Force under his command. Then, too, his experience in both racing and industry had given him an abiding confidence in his own judgment. He tended to be blunt, even with Spaatz. Where others might consult, Doolittle acted.

Here again, changed circumstances permitted quick judgments. This was the case when Doolittle strolled into the office of Major General William E. Kepner, chief of Eighth Air Force Fighter Command, looked at a framed motto that declared: "Our job is to bring the bombers back," and promptly announced that this idea was all wrong. The mission of Kepner's fighters, according to Doolittle, was to destroy the Luftwaffe, even if this meant leaving the bombers unescorted at times, for every German fighter destroyed, even if it was shot down out of sight of the bomber formation, was one fewer to attack the Flying Fortresses and Liberators.

Doolittle thus reversed the policy of close escort that Eaker had adopted. In the early days, Eaker's fighter commander, Brigadier General Frank O'D. ("Monk") Hunter, had argued in favor of fighter sweeps designed to bring the enemy to battle and shoot down his Messer-schmitts and Focke-Wulfs. Eaker had insisted, however, that the P-47s stay with the bombers as long as fuel permitted. The argument had been largely academic, since the aerial battlefield lay over Germany, beyond the range of fighters with the auxiliary fuel tanks then available. Never-theless, Eaker replaced Hunter with Kepner, who as far as possible tied his fighters to the bombing formations.

Actually, Kepner could not have done otherwise. To have sent his few P-51Bs out searching for enemy fighters, for example, could have resulted in disaster during the weeks when the Eighth Air Force was recovering from the effects of the second Schweinfurt attack. Now, since Doolittle's coming, the number of Mustangs was increasing, fighter command was receiving satisfactory auxiliary tanks for the newer P-47s and additional nose guns were appearing on the B-17s and B-24s. Dis-tant cover of the strike formations had become feasible.

During the early weeks of 1944, Eighth Air Force operations un-derwent a subtle change under Doolittle's command. The recovery from Schweinfurt was now complete. Emphasis shifted to preparation for fu-ture operations, including daytime participation in the Battle of Berlin, which Harris's night bombers had already launched.

8. Big Week

The first bombing missions flown after Doolittle's arrival continued to require the use of Oboe for navigation and Mickey Mouse, as the new H2X radar had come to be called, for attacking through the overcast that blanketed much of northern Europe during winter. On the new B-17Gs, the H2X dome was at first crowded behind the chin turret, which now afforded additional protection against head-on fighter attack. In the Liberators, which now boasted a power turret in the nose, it was necessary to remove the belly turret in order to install the antenna for Mickey Mouse, a practice eventually adopted for the B-17Gs. The aircraft fitted out with H2X, and sometimes Oboe as well, served as pathfinders, marking the target with parachute flares for the other aircraft in the formation.

Because H2X was new and tended to break down, Eighth Air Force planners elected to use it as a back-up for the Norden sight when they launched a force of 650 Liberators and Flying Fortresses against aircraft plants deep in Germany, including the Focke-Wulf factory at Oschersle-

Escorting P-51s crisscross over a B-17

ben. The weather during this 11 January raid proved so bad that part of
the fighter escort could not find its assigned bombardment groups, and
some of the bombers had to turn back. After flying for hundreds of miles
through rain and cloud, 174 B-17s, escorted by only 49 P-51s and a
handful of P-38s, found Oschersleben bathed in sunshine, and bombed
using the Norden sight. Had the skies not cleared, the attack would
have been impossible, because a rocket fired from an Me 110 downed
the pathfinder, one of 34 bombers destroyed. The Mustang pilots,

though too few in number to cover a badly scattered formation, fought gallantly, and one of them, James Howard, received his Medal of Honor for this day's action.

Meanwhile, another bombardment group, unable to verify a recall signal, attacked a Messerschmitt assembly plant near Brunswick, inflicting structural damage to most of the buildings. As the Fortresses tried to return to England they encountered a 90-mile-per-hour head wind that prolonged their exposure to German fighters. Of 20 B-17s in one of the defensive boxes that delivered this attack, seven failed to return.

Losses for the 11 January battles numbered 60, the same total as for the second Schweinfurt mission. This time, however, no period of recuperation proved necessary, for reinforcements had enabled the command to absorb casualties that would have crippled it just three months earlier. The key to German success, moreover, had been weather, which had caused the recall of part of the raiding force and deprived the remainder of adequate fighter protection.

The replacements that swelled the ranks of the Eighth Air Force had much to learn, and learned quickly. Statistics showed that many of the new pilots were experiencing overheating engines and even blown cylinders that forced them to turn back short of the target. Colonel Cass Hough, a sort of troubleshooter at large, investigated and found that the recent arrivals had been taught to open the cooling flaps on the engine cowl too soon, increasing drag as they climbed to the assembly area. This increased drag required more power, causing the very problem that the flaps were supposed to prevent.

The newcomers sometimes could cut their teeth on a milk run such as the strikes against V-1 launch facilities under construction in the Calais area. Attacks upon towns like Kiel in northwestern Germany provided needed experience and also enabled the Americans to make use of Gee or G-H to defy the overcast. As February wore away, time came for the series of raids that the newspapers called Big Week.

This series of daylight attacks began on 20 February, when a thousand Eighth Air Force bombers took off to attack a dozen aircraft plants, most of them in the Brunswick-Oschersleben area, where losses had been so heavy on 11 January. This time, however, the weather was clear and the fighter protection overwhelming. Fifty-nine bombers had to turn back because of mechanical problems, but of the 941 making the attacks, 920 returned to England, though some were damaged and had dead or wounded on board. The first Eighth Air Force contributions to

Big Week were among the most successful raids of the war in terms of aircraft lost, but the day's fighting demanded great courage and resourcefulness from several individuals.

A B-17 flown by First Lieutenant William R. Lawley entered its final run with bomb bay doors open, but the release mechanism jammed, forcing the pilot to turn away from the target with some two-tons of high explosive still on board. From 12 o'clock, several German fighters knifed into the formation, scoring a direct hit with a 20-mm shell in the cockpit of Lawley's plane. The explosion drove shell fragments into his face and killed the copilot. The Flying Fortress nosed over, but Lawley regained control despite being almost blinded from his own blood. A check over the interphone disclosed that the burst of fire had raked the length of the fuselage, wounding seven other men and also setting an engine on fire. Realizing that the flames might spread and detonate the bomb load, Lawley ordered the crew to jump, but two of the men were so badly hurt that they could not use their parachutes. The others chose to stay with the plane.

Intelligence officers plan a Berlin raid, February 1944

Fifteenth Air Force B-24 waits for a path to
be cleared

Lawley's crew may have regretted this decision almost immediately, for as he dropped out of formation to attempt a crash landing, another fighter set a second engine on fire. Fortunately, the second blaze burned itself out, the engine kept running, and the bombardier managed to jettison the bombs, so that the battered aircraft had at least a slim chance of reaching England. First Lieutenant Harry Mason, the bombardier, then took the place of the dead copilot, handling the controls whenever the wounded pilot lapsed into unconsciousness.

Lawley revived as the bomber limped across the Channel, but before he found an airfield, one of the three functioning engines ran out of fuel. Peering through the shattered windscreen, he saw an airstrip ahead and had begun a hurried approach when another engine quit. The control column shook in his hands, the bomber hung on the brink of a stall, but Lawley made a successful crash landing. For bringing back the plane and the wounded men on board, Lawley received the Medal of Honor, one of three awarded that day.

The other two awards commemorated the heroism of Second Lieutenant Walter Truemper and Sergeant Archie Mathies. After bombing an aircraft plant at Leipzig, their B-17 took a direct hit in the cockpit and began drifting out of formation. The bombardier called for everyone to bail out, then jumped himself, but the other crewmen remained with the plane. Truemper, the navigator, and Mathies, the flight engineer and belly gunner, entered the cabin and discovered that the plane remained flyable, even though the copilot was dead and the pilot badly wounded. Both Mathies and Truemper had occasionally sat at the controls of a multiengine plane, though neither was a qualified pilot. Spelled at times by other members of the crew, they guided the bomber back to their base in England.

The group commander went aloft in a Flying Fortress to lead the men down but could not make radio contact. When the control tower got through to the damaged bomber, Mathies and Truemper were told to head the plane out to sea and have everyone jump. They replied that, after all those who were able had parachuted, they would attempt to land and save the pilot's life. Following instructions radioed from the tower, the two men, who had never landed any kind of airplane, made two unsuccessful approaches. On the third, as they tried to line up the bomber with the runway, they apparently throttled back too abruptly. The nose came up, causing the plane to stall and crash short of the airfield. Both Truemper and Mathies were killed instantly, and while the wounded pilot survived the wreck, he died shortly afterward.

Weather disrupted the strikes planned for the following day, though pathfinders used H2X to hit aircraft plants at Brunswick. The attack caused little damage. The weather on 22 February proved too much even for Curtis LeMay, who had to cancel a mission against Schweinfurt because dense clouds prevented the formation from assembling over England. A total of 466 Eighth Air Force bombers headed toward Germany, but only 99 found and bombed their assigned targets, while 111 could find nothing worth bombing. The Fifteenth Air Force, however, launched a strike from Italy that battered the Messerschmitt factory at Regensburg.

German fighters claimed 54 bombers on the 22d, 41 of them from Eighth Air Force formations. Because of the differences in cruising speed, Doolittle's planners had to time the progress of the fighter escort so that it would meet the bombers near the target, where the danger had always been greatest. As a result, most of the fast fighters took off later than the bomber formations to which they were assigned. Protection, therefore, was strongest over the target and weakest early in the mission. Realizing this, the Germans jumped the day's formations as soon as possible, scoring some easy victories and forcing American planners to adjust their coverage.

Weather proved so grim on the 23d that Doolittle kept his bombers on the ground. On the next day, however, the Eighth Air Force bombed targets from Tutow in Poland to Gotha and Schweinfurt, deep in Germany, while the Fifteenth attacked Steyr, Austria. Steyr, like Schweinfurt, was a center for the manufacture of ball bearings, but the purpose of most of the day's seven attacks was to damage aircraft plants. One of the groups assigned to bomb an Me 110 factory at Gotha suffered a bizarre accident, when the lead bombardier experienced oxygen failure and in losing consciousness inadvertently released his bombs too soon. The other aircraft followed his example, but notable accuracy by another group helped compensate for the error.

RAF Bomber Command, which had prefaced Big Week with a strike against Leipzig on the night of 19 February and then hit Stuttgart, joined in on the 24th by raiding Schweinfurt. At Casablanca, Eaker had proposed that the Royal Air Force bomb by night targets that the Eighth Air Force had set ablaze during the day. In this instance however, the daytime bombing had been inaccurate, hitting a jam factory, a producer of malt extract and a firm manufacturing gelatin, besides setting fires at the ball-bearing plants. For their part, the men of Bomber Command apparently conducted the usual city-busting attack. Had the combined raids taken place in October 1943, disruption of German industry would have been considerable, but by now the task of dispersal was under way.

Big Week came to an end on 25 February, when 830 Eighth Air Force heavy bombers divided their attention among four cities—Augsburg, Stuttgart, Regensburg and Fürth. Aerial photographs indicated severe damage to the Messerschmitt complex at Regensburg, but the company had been dispersing its activities to other locations ever since the August 1943 attack, and the evidence of the camera was therefore misleading. Once again winter closed in over northern Europe, halting long-range missions for about a week.

The 31 bombers that failed to return from these final missions of Big Week swelled the total number of American aircraft lost to 216 bombers and 28 fighters, with about 2,600 airmen killed, wounded or captured. During this same period, Bomber Harris sent some 2,400 sorties against five cities—Leipzig, Stuttgart, Schweinfurt, Steyr and Augsburg—losing 157 bombers. The loss rate for both daylight and night raids lay between 6 and 7 percent.

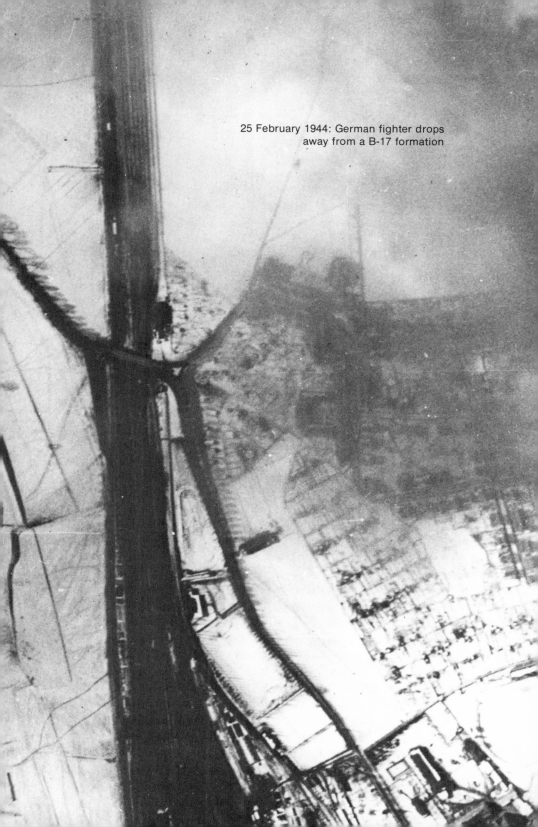

25 February 1944: German fighter drops
away from a B-17 formation

The effects of Big Week were difficult to assess. U.S. intelligence consistently underestimated both German aircraft production capacity and the ability of the aviation industry to recover from aerial bombardment. Messerschmitt production declined at Regensburg and Augsburg, for instance, but rebounded to previous levels within 30 to 90 days. The greatest damage done the Luftwaffe may well have been the fighters shot down and the crewmen killed, for the number of German losses increased sharply as February drew to a close.

Two ball-bearing centers, Schweinfurt and Steyr, underwent attack by both American and British forces during Big Week, as did Stuttgart, the site of another factory that turned out the antifriction devices. The strikes had little effect on aircraft production, however, for Albert Speer was doing his work with great efficiency. By using substitutes in less essential items and making purchases in Sweden, he had created stockpiles to see the airplane manufacturers through a crisis.

The most important aspect of Big Week was not its results but the magnitude of the effort expended. Between 20 and 25 February, Eighth Air Force Bomber Command dropped about the same weight of explosives as it had during its first year of operation. Doolittle had launched some 3,300 bomber sorties, and Fifteenth Air Force had added about 500, while the total fighter sorties exceeded 3,500. Mistakes had been made and lessons painfully learned, but the American strategic air forces in Europe had conducted an aerial campaign that would have been impossible a few months before.

9. Blasting Berlin

When Bomber Harris had launched his Battle of Berlin in November 1943, Eaker's staff had planned a daylight attack as the first American contribution to a decisive aerial campaign. Fortunately, since the Eighth Air Force lacked an escort fighter at the time, bad weather had forced cancellation of the mission, probably preventing losses that would have further delayed the command's recovery from the second Schweinfurt attack. While the Eighth Air Force gathered strength, underwent a change of command and conducted daylight strikes from Poland to Bavaria, Harris persisted in the night bombardment of the German capital.

Bomber Command had sent 444 bombers against Berlin on 18 November, the first of 16 raids involving more than 9,000 heavy-bomber sorties, most of them by the mighty Lancasters. Four-engine Handley Page Halifaxes and Short Stirlings also took part, but their lower service ceilings rendered them, especially the unwieldy Stirling, far more vulnerable than the Lancaster to both flak and fighters. Although the strike force had emerged almost unscathed from the initial attack—435 planes returned safely—losses mounted rapidly.

Once Big Week was past, the Eighth Air Force turned its eyes toward Berlin. Doolittle, who had led the first raid on Tokyo and flown as a copilot during the first strike on Rome, had hoped to fly against the third of the Axis capitals, but this was forbidden. He had received information obtained by means of Ultra, the truly top-secret Allied code-breaking operation, and the Allies could not risk his capture and the possibility that the secret might be compromised.

On 3 March the bomber force took off for Berlin, but weather forced the Liberators and Flying Fortresses to turn back. Doolittle was especially sensitive to the vagaries of the weather, possibly as the result of his record-setting transcontinental flight in 1935, during which the predicted fair skies turned out to be a combination of cloud, rain and ice. Like Eaker before him, he insisted on last-minute weather reconnaissance and had Colonel Budd Peaslee organize a scouting force, equipped with P-51s, that checked on weather conditions on the morning of scheduled raids.

Doolittle never flinched from recalling or diverting a bombing mission, for he realized that his young men were basically fair-weather airmen, trained mainly in the sunshine of the southern and southwestern United States. On one occasion, according to Doolittle biographers Lowell Thomas and Edward Jablonski, Spaatz questioned the decision, citing the day's weather forecast. Doolittle promptly replied that the meteorologist was "full of shit," pointing out that one of Peaslee's scouts was even then flying through a heavy overcast.

The bombers took off for Berlin on the following day, 4 March. Again the weather en route was bad, and Doolittle ordered the attack abandoned. But one contingent of 31 B-17s failed to hear the signal and continued toward the German capital. When General Kepner realized what was happening, he had a part of the fighter escort continue eastward to protect the bombers over the city. The lead navigator for the B-17s, First Lieutenant Malcolm Durr, located his checkpoints through gaps in the cloud, but at the target an unbroken overcast prevented use of the Norden sight. Instead, an aircraft fitted with H2X served as pathfinder. A gunner from the 100th Group, Technical Sergeant Harold Stearns, shot down the first fighter destroyed by an American over Berlin, an Me 109 that other crewmen saw burst into flame. Five of the bombers failed to return.

B-17s etch vapor trails as they drone
toward Berlin

Despite a dusting of snow at the English bases, takeoffs proceeded as planned on the 6th, and 730 bombers headed for Berlin. Escorting them were 796 fighters, including some 50 British Mustangs. In order to hit the Erkner ball-bearing plant, a major target, the raiders used a large

Bombs over Berlin, near the Tempelhof
railway station

body of water, Dummer Lake, as a reference point. Since many German fighter units employed the same landmark when assembling for the defense of the city, a savage air battle ensued.

The inexperience of recently arrived fighter units hurt the bombers, for the covering squadrons became so intent on protecting the leading and trailing elements that they failed to screen the middle of a column extending 60 miles. Enemy radar controllers on the ground massed some 100 fighters against this gap, while other FW 190s and Me 109s pinned down the escort units at the front and rear of the strike force. The prompt reaction of the radar controllers cost the Eighth Air Force almost 25 of the 69 bombers lost that day.

The copilot of an H2X-equipped pathfinder near the midpoint of the column was John C. Morgan, who had won the Medal of Honor at Oschersleben in the summer of 1943 and now wore the silver bars of a first lieutenant. As this B-17 made its bomb run on an electrical-equipment factory, flak set an engine on fire. While the crew was apprehensively estimating the damage, the bomber exploded. Concussion from the blast hurled Morgan out of the shattered cabin. He found himself falling through the frigid sky, his parachute tucked under his arm. Although the air rushing past almost tore the chute pack from his grip, he pulled the harness over his head, turned onto his back, and managed to fasten the straps. The canopy had barely filled when Morgan hit the top of a tree, cushioning his fall, and tumbled 30 feet to the ground. He landed near an antiaircraft site—another stroke of luck, since civilians

Escort commander: Colonel Hubert Zemke, of the 56th Fighter Group

who had just undergone bombing sometimes took out their anger on downed airmen—and the Luftwaffe gunners took him prisoner.

Despite losing 69 bombers shot down, three others damaged beyond repair and about 100 put temporarily out of action, Doolittle had enough men and planes to mount another massive attack on 8 March. This time some 600 bombers shaped a course for Berlin, where they bombed several targets including the Erkner ball-bearing factory. Determined to make up for their earlier error, the escorting fighters concentrated on covering the middle of the column. This grouping did not escape the notice of German radar controllers, who massed the comparatively small number of fighters that were airborne against the combat wing at the head of the bomber armada, causing confusion as these aircraft prepared to close in on their target. One group started on the wrong heading from the initial point but got back on course. Shot down during the raid were 37 bombers.

Cloud shrouded Berlin on the following day, and the exhausted German fighter pilots remained on the ground. Antiaircraft fire proved deadly, however, downing nine American planes. Unable to use the Norden sight, the bombers employed H2X, even though the sprawling city offered a radar image difficult for any but the most experienced operator to interpret.

By now cloud had settled in over all of northern Europe, forcing the American bombers either to hit the V-1 launch sites being built in France or to conduct radar strikes against aircraft plants hidden beneath the overcast. Only in the south did the skies clear, and twice large formations attacked Friedrichshafen on Lake Constance at the Swiss border. In spite of bright sunshine, Liberators from the 14th Combat Wing had to resort to radar bombing on the first raid because the defenders had placed smoke generators on rafts, floated them onto the water and let the wind spread a pall across the city. A total of 43 bombers failed to return from the first of the two strikes, but 16 of them landed in neutral Switzerland.

The second Friedrichshafen raid became a running battle, covering 100 miles, between two of the groups from the 14th Wing and roughly 175 single-engine German fighters. The raggedness of the formation—in fact, some of the Liberators found themselves over the wrong shore of Lake Constance and came under fire from Swiss batteries—and the late arrival of the escorting P-38s gave the interceptors an opportunity to attack at leisure. But they were not always successful. An Me 109 pilot, intent on claiming one of the day's 22 victims, ignored another B-24 that seemed to have been abandoned, but the crew was still on board, struggling to save the bomber. A waist gunner saw the German fighter and shot it down from a distance of about 100 yards.

American participation in the Battle of Berlin ended on 22 March with a pathfinder attack by 800 bombers. In the five missions flown during March 1944, Eighth Air Force had launched some 2,500 sorties and dropped about 4,800 tons of bombs on the German capital, roughly 40 percent of them incendiaries. Although Doolittle's B-17s and B-24s played a supporting role to Harris's bombers during this aerial campaign, the repeated daylight attacks drove home the lesson of Big Week: the Eighth Air Force could absorb punishment and fight back, giving the Allies another weapon for the destruction of Germany.

Encouraging as the American activity had been, the Battle of Berlin proved frustrating for Bomber Harris. At the outset he had stated in a matter-of-fact way that the series of attacks would level the city and cost Germany the war. The German capital, however, had survived night attacks, which burned out block after block of houses, and Eighth Air Force daytime raids that increased the overall damage, even though radar was not accurate enough for the kind of precision bombing possible with the Norden sight. Germany remained in the war, resisting the Russian advance and preparing for the impending cross-Channel attack. The effort directed against Berlin had been massive, the Allied losses greater than Harris had anticipated—almost 650 planes shot down instead of 400 to 500, and the results disappointing.

The German spirit failed to crack, despite aerial bombardment and a mounting toll of dead, maimed and missing on the eastern front. Victory had eluded Harris, who nevertheless persisted in his bombing strategy. The Nuremberg raid of 30 March, during which the night defenses organized by Josef Kammhuber downed 95 bombers, offered further evidence of both German determination and the British need for electronic countermeasures.

Control of the skies over Germany had not yet been decided, though some Luftwaffe leaders feared that the havoc visited upon Hamburg, and to a lesser degree on Berlin, lay in store for other cities. As the Battle of Berlin approached a climax, Field Marshal Erhard Milch, who as the Luftwaffe's Director General for Equipment championed the jet fighter, conceded that the capital could not endure the ordeal indefinitely. If the Allies gained control of the air, they would indeed be able

Lieutenant Colonel
Robert S. Johnson, U.S.
No. 2 ace in Europe

Close friends Capt. Don Gentile (1.) and Lt.
John T. Godfrey

to prolong interminably the agony of German cities, but for the time being the defense remained too strong to permit the Americans and British this freedom of action.

In daylight, at least, tipping the balance in favor of the offense rested with a group of young fighter pilots like Robert S. Johnson, who while a child had made his first flight in the passenger compartment of a Ford trimotor. Johnson learned fighter tactics in Hubert Zemke's 56th Fighter Group and amassed a total of 27 victories, flying various models of P-47. Another of Zemke's pilots, Francis ("Gabby") Gabreski, became the leading American ace of the European Theater of Operations, destroying 28 enemy planes. Since he spoke fluent Polish, the Pennsylvania-born Gabreski left the 56th Fighter Group to fly for a time with a Royal Air Force unit made up of refugees from Poland. Shot down in the summer of 1944, he spent the rest of the war in a prison camp. Zemke, too, was shot down and imprisoned, but not before he had accounted for 17.75 German aircraft, while flying the P-47 and later the Mustang.

The leading P-51 ace was George E. Preddy, killed in December 1944 when American troops mistook his airplane for an Me 109 and shot him down. On the very day he died, Preddy scored his 24th and 25th victories, surpassing by one the total of John C. Meyer, who also flew the Mustang. Singled out for praise by Prime Minister Churchill, who described them as the Damon and Pythias of the air war, were two close friends, Don Gentile, who shot down 21.8 planes, and his wingman, John T. Godfrey, with 18 victories. Gentile flew with one of the Eagle Squadrons, shooting down two Germans before transferring from the Royal Air Force to the 4th Fighter Group. Godfrey, an American who had begun his war service with the Royal Canadian Air Force, served two combat tours, was shot down during the second, and ended the war a captive of the enemy.

These men and others like them—the Walker Mahurins, Raymond Wetmores and David Schillings of the Eighth Air Force Fighter Command—brought to reality the premonition of defeat felt by Hermann Göring when the first American fighters appeared over Berlin. For the time being, however, Berlin and the other German cities enjoyed a respite, as Doolittle's airmen joined in preparations for the forthcoming Allied invasion of France.

10. The Transportation Plan

The Eighth Air Force figured prominently in the plans that were approved by General Dwight D. Eisenhower, the Allied Supreme Commander, for the invasion of Europe. The overriding mission assigned Doolittle's airmen was to prevent the Luftwaffe from intervening during the amphibious assault and the expansion of the beachhead. The secondary mission was to attack the German transportation network. Even so, General Spaatz managed to obtain approval for a few daylight precision attacks on oil refineries and plants producing synthetic gasoline, the idea being to deny fuel to the German fighters, but both Eighth and Fifteenth Air Force bombers had to concentrate upon disrupting the enemy's transportation network. The B-17s and B-24s joined medium and light bombers in tearing up rail lines in France to isolate the coming battlefield, though the heavies also hit rail complexes in eastern Europe, where the Germans were massing against the inexorable Russian advance.

Fighters played the decisive role in neutralizing German air power

99

and severing the transportation arteries. On 20 May, for example, some 1,200 British and American fighters fanned out across France and western Germany, shooting up trains and daring the Luftwaffe to intervene. American P-47s and British Hawker Typhoons proved especially deadly, with the Thunderbolts knocking out bridges with half-ton, high-explosive bombs.

Transportation attacks behind the invasion beaches paralyzed a German army that relied upon highways and rail lines to move reinforcements and heavy equipment to the Channel coast. Tactical bombers flown by the Ninth Air Force, rather than the Eighth Air Force heavies, achieved the decisive results in the final days before the invasion, destroying every bridge leading across the River Seine and preventing German forces north of that stream from moving to oppose the landings. Thanks to the working of the Transportation Plan, as it was called, the Allies could reinforce their beachhead by sea faster than the enemy could strengthen his defenses by land.

Awaiting the signal to take off, B-17 crewmen soak up some sun

Although successful in a military sense, the attacks on roads and rail lines caused some casualties among civilians in the occupied countries. Despite the personal tragedy involved, the general populace accepted death or injury as part of the price of deliverance from German oppression. Indeed, the bombing gave French trainmen an excuse to desert the service of their enemy.

German airdromes in western Europe also came under attack. Heavy bombers from the Eighth and Fifteenth Air Forces took part in the airfield strikes, with Doolittle sending some 400 of these aircraft against Paris airfields on a single day, while Italian-based B-24s and B-17s probed southern France. When Adolf Galland, in command of Luftwaffe fighters, attempted to deploy his units westward to contest the Allied landings on 6 June, most of the airstrips that he had planned to use were cratered by bombs.

The Eighth Air Force also helped pave the way for the Normandy landings by battering the coastal defenses. Prior to D-Day, the Flying Fortresses and Liberators conducted four major attacks on segments of the Atlantic Wall, the batteries and other German fortifications built to oppose the invasion. During the first strike, Doolittle insisted on the use of H2X, as a form of practice for a predawn attack during D-Day itself. Results were poor, though accuracy improved in the later raids, thanks to visual aiming. These preparatory bombings, and heavier attacks by Royal Air Force Bomber Command on the coastal defenses, did little damage to the Atlantic Wall, though they may have to some extent demoralized the defenders.

Both Eighth Air Force and Bomber Command returned early on D-Day morning, bombing the invasion beaches before the landing craft touched down. More than 1,000 B-17s and B-24s conducted a massive pathfinder attack on four of the five chosen beaches, dropping almost 3,000 tons of bombs, which were instantaneously fuzed in order to avoid digging craters that would impede the assault forces. Bomber Command also scattered Window to confuse German radar.

After helping Allied ground forces seize a foothold on the continent of Europe, the heavy bombers of the Eighth Air Force attempted to lay down a carpet of bombs that would stun the German defenders, enabling American troops to break out from the beachhead and overrun the Cotentin Peninsula. Lieutenant General Omar Bradley, the ground commander, planned to have his infantrymen poised at the edge of the area to be bombed, ready to move forward before the Germans had re-

Bombers hit ferrying facilities at Rouen

Colonel Francis Gabreski,
Flight Officer Steven
Gerick—June 1944

covered from the detonation of three or four thousand tons of explosives. Rapid, aggressive movement held the key to success. "If they get set," Bradley told his commanders, "we go right back to this hedge fighting"—the area was laced with barricadelike hedgerows—"and you can't make any speed." Repeating that "this thing must be bold," he arranged to have his soldiers take up positions within 1,200 yards of a highway that marked the near edge of the impact area. As a safety factor, low-flying fighter-bombers would attack just beyond this road, with the heavy bombers withholding their explosives for a distance of 250 yards.

The day selected for this carpet bombing, 24 July, dawned gloomy, and the heavy overcast refused to dissipate. Air Chief Marshal Sir Trafford Leigh-Mallory, representing Eisenhower's supreme headquarters, visited Normandy that morning, decided that the weather would prevent accurate bombing and called off the attack. But by the time the message reached England, almost the entire strike force had already taken off. A recall went out immediately but failed to reach the 1,600 heavy bombers thundering across the Channel. Most of these B-17s and B-24s could not locate the highway and other landmarks that lay hidden beneath the cloud, and hence they refused to attack. But about 300 bombers found gaps in the overcast, through which they dropped more than 650 tons of bombs.

103

The results of the attack were tragic. One bombardier was preparing to release his explosives when an unopened bundle of Chaff, dropped from another plane, stuck the nose turret. He flinched, toggling the bombs, which destroyed two American aircraft parked at an airstrip below and killed the crew members on board.

Another bombardier accidentally dropped part of his bomb load early because of a faulty release mechanism. Fifteen other aircraft in the formation followed his example, depositing their high explosive and fragmentation bombs 2,000 yards short of the highway that served as a safety marker. Sixteen American soldiers died as a result of this accident, and 60 were wounded.

Major General J. Lawton Collins, responsible for carrying out the plan, realized that the attack had alerted the Germans, but nevertheless decided to try carpet bombing again the following day, hitting the enemy at mid-morning instead of in early afternoon. A weather reconnaissance plane checked the area and reported good visibility. Army artillery fired red smoke shells to mark the target area, and the front-line infantrymen withdrew 1,500 yards from the highway before laying down brightly colored cloth panels to mark their positions. For almost three hours, 559 fighter-bombers, 380 mediums and 1,507 Flying Fortresses and Liberators tried to pulverize the area. Although the bombing was generally accurate, both Eighth Air Force heavies and mediums from the Ninth dropped high-explosive and fragmentation bombs within American lines. As had happened on the previous day, most of the misdirected ordnance fell upon the 30th Infantry Division, wounding 380 men and killing 102, among them Lieutenant General Lesley J. McNair, chief of Army Ground Forces. In proposing Operation Cobra, as the carpet bombing was called, General Bradley had warned that his units would have to be prepared to accept heavy losses. The nature of the attack—to avoid enemy antiaircraft fire, the bombers had to approach from behind American lines instead of flying parallel to them—made it inevitable that some of those losses would result from American bombs.

The effect of Cobra on German units was mixed. In some sectors the enemy moved beyond the highway when the Americans pulled back, thus escaping the heaviest of the bombing, and opened fire when the infantry moved forward. Other advancing units found the Germans stunned, disorganized and incapable of resisting. Among the hardest-hit German units was an armored division, whose commander, General Fritz Bayerlein, climbed a stone tower, surveyed the battlefield and reported that the landscape resembled the surface of the moon. Telephone lines had been severed, tanks half-buried and 88-mm guns toppled from their mounts, but the general nonetheless managed to rally the survivors from his division.

Cobra had not achieved all General Bradley had anticipated. In some places, bomb craters had slowed the American advance, and a few German units had emerged intact to fight savagely. When the day ended, the enemy still controlled several key strongpoints. General Collins decided, however, to commit his reserve, which on the following day succeeded in breaking through.

Far more successful were the heavy bomber strikes during November 1944 against German fortifications at Metz and Thionville, just west of the Franco-German border. To avoid friendly casualties, Lieutenant General George S. Patton, Jr., demanded a four-mile zone between the targets hit by these aircraft and his own troops. As a result, most of the bombers could use H2X in attacking through an overcast without fear of hitting friendly forces. The bombing, though it caused little damage to the defensive structures, proved heavy enough to stagger the Germans manning them.

One of the B-17s on the Metz-Thionville raid was *Lady Janet*, flown by First Lieutenant Donald Gott and his copilot, Second Lieutenant William Metzger. Since the dense overcast kept the crew from recognizing landmarks that would have guided them close enough to the fortified areas for the radar attack, they began searching for a secondary target. During this quest the bomber flew within range of a radar-controlled flak battery hidden beneath the cloud. German gunners knocked out three of the plane's engines, one of them trailing a plume of flame that extended all the way to the tail surfaces. Shell fragments severed the radio operator's arm, but Metzger managed to apply a tourniquet. After jettisoning the bombs over German territory and ordering the able-bodied crewmen to jump, the pilot and copilot attempted to crash-land in order to save the wounded man. Just 100 feet from safety, flame from the burning engine reached a fuel tank and the B-17 exploded, killing the three men. Both Gott and Metzger were judged deserving of the Medal of Honor.

A week after the Metz-Thionville bombing, B-17s and B-24s attacked German fortifications around Aachen. To prevent repetition of the Cobra accidents, the soldiers marked their forward positions with both ground panels and barrage balloons, while firing smoke shells fuzed

German fighter trails a B-17 on its
bombing run

to explode in the air at specified intervals along the front line. In addition, radio beacons signaled the bombers the moment they passed over the friendly troops. Thanks to these precautions, only one bomb fell short of the target, and it caused no casualties.

After the German counteroffensive through the Ardennes Forest, beginning the Battle of the Bulge, Eighth Air Force bombers again went to the aid of the ground forces, attacking airfields and transportation centers that supported the German attack on Bastogne, Belgium, a vital American redoubt near the Luxembourg border. The Germans attacked on 16 December 1944, their preparations cloaked by fog and cloud, but in a week the skies had cleared enough to permit the Flying Fortresses and Liberators to join in the battle.

Leading a Christmas Eve attack on German airfields east of the Rhine was Fred Castle, one of Eaker's original staff, who had recently been promoted to brigadier general. German fighters jumped the bomber column over Belgium before the Mustang escort arrived. When the enemy struck, Castle's B-17G, a war-weary craft that had been returned to service to help meet the Bulge emergency, experienced engine trouble and had to struggle to stay in formation. Fire from the

Me 109s crippled the bomber, which began losing altitude. Ordinarily Castle would have ordered the bombs jettisoned to lighten the aircraft and reduce the danger of explosion, but he refused because he was above Allied-held territory. He held the plane steady so that the surviving crew members could parachute, but this left him an easy target for the Germans, one of whom shot the wing off the bomber. Six of the crew managed to escape, but Castle died in the crash. The posthumous award of the Medal of Honor paid tribute to his courage.

The Eighth Air Force and RAF Bomber Command also had to divert men, bombs and aircraft from the campaign against Germany in order to take part in Operation Crossbow, the attempt to destroy the sites from which the enemy launched his V-weapons against Britain and later against the captured port of Antwerp. Crossbow had begun well before the invasion, with American and British heavy bombers joining tactical aircraft in battering the concrete bunkers and launching ramps that were appearing along the French coast. This bombing delayed the introduction of the V-1 by perhaps three months, so that none of these buzz bombs came gliding down upon English ports crowded with troops and invasion shipping. One week after D-Day, however, the enemy launched his first V-1 against England, and soon the heavy bombers resumed flying Crossbow missions.

July and August 1944 proved to be the most violent months in Hitler's V-1 offensive, with as many as 160 of the weapons reaching the English coast in a single 24-hour period and more than 800 in one week. Besides helping to attack the V-1 launch sites, Doolittle's men bombed storage depots, fuel dumps, and plants producing the liquid oxygen required for the V-2 rocket. Thanks to excellent intelligence from agents in occupied Europe and neutral Sweden, the bombing of facilities essential to the V-2 program could begin before the first of these weapons exploded in England.

Although aerial bombing delayed introduction of the vengeance weapons, this form of attack could not put an end to their use. The V-1 offensive diminished after Allied forces captured western France, but both buzz bombs and rockets continued to fall until late March 1945, when ground forces pushed the enemy beyond range of the British Isles. Easily camouflaged, widely dispersed and protected by flak batteries, the individual launch sites proved difficult to locate and attack; in addition, the enemy released some V-1s from obsolete bombers based along the North Sea coast.

Crossbow gave rise to a joint attempt by the U.S. Navy and U.S.

B-17 attacks a V-1 fuel plant at
Pennemünde, Germany

Army Air Forces to convert obsolete bombers into guided missiles for attacks on V-1 launch complexes and similar targets ringed by antiaircraft batteries. The inspiration for this project may have been an experimental television-guided bomb tested unsuccessfully by the Eighth Air Force in February 1944. The basic principle behind the converted bomber was, in any case, the same as that of the guided bomb. Television installed in the nose of the war-weary B-17 or B-24 enabled a controller in another aircraft to guide the drone into its target. A volunteer pilot flew the aircraft, which was usually filled with a combination of high explosive and jellied gasoline, until the remote controller took charge, then parachuted to safety.

Such was the theoretical procedure. In practice, the arming and guidance circuitry proved complex and dangerous. One of the bombers exploded in midair when the pilot threw the arming switch in preparation for bailing out. Killed in this accident was a young naval aviator, Joseph P. Kennedy, Jr., whose brother John would become President of the United States. Another of the bombers failed to respond to guidance signals and headed toward a coastal town before crashing harmlessly. Despite some hits on enemy installations, the project, which carried the inappropriate name Aphrodite, was canceled. A successful television-guided weapon lay some years in the future.

Regensburg was the first shuttle-
bombing target

11. Shuttle Bombing

The first attempt at shuttle bombing by the Eighth Air Force occurred on 17 August 1943, when Curtis LeMay led a strike on Regensburg, then continued on to airfields in Tunisia, where his B-17s were to prepare for another raid during the return flight. This attack would complete a "shuttle" between England and Africa. But when LeMay landed in Tunisia, he found neither the repair facilities nor the crew quarters that had been promised him. Several badly damaged B-17s had to be abandoned in North Africa, as those aircraft sound enough for the long flight made their way back to the British Isles, flying well out to sea to avoid German fighters.

Despite the failure of this mission, the result of abysmally bad planning by the Eighth Air Force staff, General Arnold pushed for the adoption of shuttle bombing, using Russian bases. During 1943, as continuing losses threatened the future of daylight bombing, the Commanding General, Army Air Forces, looked upon the Russian bases as a means of diluting the fighter defenses of western Europe. The enemy had massed his squadrons in this area, attacking the bomber formations from the moment the raiders entered German airspace until they departed en route back to their bases in England. If Ira Eaker, then in command of the Eighth Air Force, could hit Germany from east as well as west, Reichsmarschall Göring would have to divide his fighter forces, reducing the likelihood of crippling losses such as those the bomber force had suffered on 17 August during the attacks on Regensburg and Schweinfurt.

The establishment of the Fifteenth Air Force in Italy late in 1943 increased the potential value of Russian bases. Heavy bombers could take off from the vicinity of Foggia, in southern Italy, bomb aircraft plants in eastern Germany, rearm and refuel in the Soviet Union, and hit similar targets during the return flight. A further strain would be imposed on the Luftwaffe fighter force, thus compelled to fight on three fronts—east, south and west—to protect the factories that produced its aircraft.

Since the neutralization of the Luftwaffe was a key element in the preparations for D-Day, the idea of using Russian airfields exerted a continuing fascination for the Americans. As a result, when Joseph Stalin, the Soviet dictator, expressed approval of the plan, his negotiators obtained a number of concessions that would have been unthinkable a few years earlier. For example, General Arnold instructed Carl Spaatz, commander of the strategic air forces in Europe, to furnish the Red Air Force with a Norden bombsight, a device withheld from the British as recently as 1940.

Throughout the negotiations, the Russians sought to limit the amount of contact between the local populace and the Americans, whose aircraft would operate from Mirgorod, Piryatin and Poltava, the three bases in the Ukraine made available for the undertaking. Instead of allowing American engineers to repair these airstrips and extend the runways, the Russians insisted that their own labor units do the work. The American negotiators stated that U.S. Strategic Air Forces in Europe would have to send 2,100 mechanics, administrators and communications specialists to operate the three bases and man the headquarters at Poltava. Stalin refused. Suspicious of foreigners and determined to keep the number of Americans small and their influence easily contained, he imposed a ceiling of 1,200.

In charge of the Americans sent to the Russian bases was Colonel Alfred A. Kessler, whom the Russians called "Uncle Ugly." Scarcely had he moved into the headquarters at Poltava when security men discov-

112

ered a dozen German bombs concealed beneath the structure, ready to be detonated by a radio signal from an aircraft. The giant booby trap was disarmed without incident.

Getting along with the Russians proved difficult. Differences in language and custom resulted in friction, and the Soviet officers worried about having their men politically contaminated by the ideas contained in American magazines. Kessler recalled that his Russian counterpart, Major General A. R. Perminov, insisted that the foreigners keep their publications out of Russian hands, but would then read the forbidden material in the privacy of the colonel's quarters.

Occasional fistfights broke out, one of them triggered by a group of Americans who taught a waitress in the dining hall to respond with an obscenity to any question asked in English. Unfortunately, she repeated this remark to a visiting American general who, irate as only a general can be, reported the incident to Perminov. In the course of the Russian's investigation, the local Red Army garrison learned the story, and several of them went looking for the Americans responsible. Fortunately for the project, Kessler and Perminov got along splendidly and were able to restore a measure of harmony.

Plans had called for Doolittle's Eighth Air Force to launch Operation Frantic, as the shuttle bombing was called. D-Day was fast approaching, however, so the Fifteenth Air Force, commanded by Major General Nathan F. Twining, flew the first mission. General Eaker, who had flown on the first B-17 strike against a target in Europe, was in one of the 130 Flying Fortresses dispatched from Italy on the early morning of 2 June 1944. Escorted by P-51s, the bombers attacked the railway yards at Debrecen, Hungary, carrying out one of the strikes on German transportation intended to prevent the redeployment of forces to meet the impending invasion of France. Over the target, one of the B-17s suddenly caught fire, either from flak or from a fuel leak, and exploded in midair, killing everyone on board. This was the only bomber lost over Hungary.

At the border between Hungary and Russia, clouds were beginning to gather. Realizing that the Americans at Poltava and the other airfields did not yet have radio beacons on which the formation might home, Eaker ordered the planes below the overcast. Well ahead of the B-17s, the 64 Mustangs, led by Colonel Chester Sluder, were groping toward Piryatin, red lights glowing on many an instrument panel to indicate that fuel was almost gone. Luck intervened when Sluder spotted a rail

Fifteenth Air Force B-17s festoon the
sky with vapor trails

line, gambled that it led toward Piryatin, turned in that direction and
reached the base without losing a single airplane.

The B-17s landed in the rain at Mirgorod and Poltava. The surface
at the latter field was especially tricky, since the wet grass extended
through the holes in the metal planking that formed the landing surface.
Eaker's plane, with Captain Leslie Gates at the controls, blew both tires
but skidded to a stop at the very end of the runway.

During the round of celebrations following the successful mission,
Eaker had an opportunity to examine the defense of Poltava. He did not
like what he saw. Antiaircraft batteries with women crews had dug in
around the field, but they had no heavy guns. The interceptors assigned
to the bases were day fighters, some of them Bell P-39s supplied under
lend-lease. Poltava, and presumably the other fields as well, remained
vulnerable to night or high-altitude attack. Since German radio propagandists predicted the destruction of the American aircraft that had
just landed in Russia, and the enemy had a sizable force of bombers

Fighter ace Lieutenant Duane Beeson
chats with a crew member

within striking range, Eaker hoped to depart for Italy as soon as the weather permitted. Spaatz, however, wanted him to remain in Russia until after D-Day. As a result, the force took off on the morning of 6 June, while the Allies were fighting for the Normandy beaches, bombed an airfield at Galatz, Rumania, and returned to the Russian airfields. German fighters downed two Mustangs, though one of the pilots survived and was taken prisoner. Not until 11 June did the Fifteenth Air Force contingent bomb Focsani airfield, near Bucharest, and continue on to Italy.

This mission had a disastrous effect on Operation Frantic and on the Eighth Air Force. The one Flying Fortress shot down at Bucharest carried some 500 photographs taken during the first shuttle mission. These helped the enemy plan the reconnaissance flights that pinpointed the location of the main base at Poltava. On 21 June, when Eaker launched the next bomber force, the Germans were ready.

Entrusted to lead the first Frantic mission from England was Colonel Archie Old, whose force consisted of 163 B-17s escorted by 70 P-51s. Old remained with a huge striking force bound for Berlin, then changed course near the capital and bombed a synthetic fuel plant near Ruhland. A few bombers became separated and attacked targets in Poland. One Mustang and none of the bombers went down over Germany, though Old's plane took a flak hit in the wing, causing fuel to leak from an auxiliary tank. The worst moments, however, lay ahead.

Once again bad weather closed in, but by now radio beacons marked the location of the airfields. Even so, seven Flying Fortresses came down short of their destination, either stumbling upon Russian airdromes and landing or plowing furrows in wheat fields. While ap-

115

P-51s of the Fifteenth Air Force fly
high over Italy

proaching one of these unauthorized landing fields, the gunners of one B-17 had to open fire in order to discourage a pair of Soviet fighters that seemed intent upon attacking. When the commander of the interceptor unit heard how his young pilots had dived away from the tracers, he found it uproariously funny. He saw nothing unusual about the fighter pilots' preparing to attack; in fact, he would have been furious if they had not. What amused him was their allowing the Americans to frighten them.

In spite of the fuel leak, Old reached Poltava early in the evening and landed safely. High in the substratosphere behind him was a Heinkel He 177 reconnaissance plane piloted by Hans Mueller. From the glass-enclosed pressurized cabin, he and his crew watched the activity below, then returned to an airfield at German-held Minsk, where they reported that the Americans were ripe for attack.

Old and Kessler were attending a banquet when word came that German planes had been sighted approaching Poltava. Sirens warned the bomber crews to take cover, though some of them had become so accustomed to German nuisance raids against England that they ignored the alarm. Meanwhile, a mixed force of Junkers Ju 88 and Heinkel He 111 twin-engine bombers, led by Colonel Wilhelm Antrup, was closing on the airfield. The escorting Me 109s disposed of a handful of Red Air Force fighters that happened upon the German raiders, and shortly after midnight target-marking flares began bursting over the airfield.

For almost an hour, enemy planes methodically bombed the airfield, and when these aircraft left, another wave appeared, continuing the attack for another 30 minutes or more. Antrup's raiders dumped 110 tons of bombs on the airdrome, destroying 43 Flying Fortresses while damaging 26 of the bombers and 15 Mustangs. The attack claimed two American lives, one man killed on the early morning of 22 June and another who later died of wounds suffered at that time. The defenses of Poltava proved even more porous than Eaker had feared.

Following the Poltava disaster, Spaatz's first concern was to get the surviving bombers and escort fighters out of the Soviet Union as quickly as possible. These aircraft departed on 26 June, bombed a synthetic fuel plant in Poland, and landed in Italy, where they flew one mission with the Fifteenth Air Force before returning to England. Rather than risk additional heavy bombers until the defenses were strengthened at the bases, Spaatz shuttled Lightnings and Mustangs between Italy and Russia. The fighters shot up rail lines and airfields en route.

The Eighth Air Force launched its second shuttle mission on 6 August. Flying Fortresses escorted by Mustangs bombed an aircraft plant at Gdynia and delivered a strike against oil refineries at Trzebinia, both in Poland, and later flew to Italy, hitting Rumanian airfields en route. The last Frantic bombing mission flown by Doolittle's command occurred in mid-September, when the Flying Fortresses and their escort hit Chemnitz, Germany, en route to the Soviet Union, bombed a Hungarian steel mill on the way to Italy, and completed the triangle by returning to England.

One shuttle mission remained, however, before the project collapsed amid political controversy. On 1 August 1944, convinced that the advancing Red Army would be bound to come to his aid, General Tadeusz Bor-Komorovski gave orders for an uprising by his Warsaw underground forces against the occupying Germans. The Soviets, who supported a Polish Communist faction, halted on the outskirts of the city, while the vengeful Germans attempted to exterminate Bor's insurgents.

President Roosevelt and Prime Minister Churchill searched about for some means of helping the Poles. Since B-17s loaded with arms and supplies could not fly to Warsaw and back to England, a Frantic mission offered the best hope, but such an undertaking required Soviet approval. The Russians refused, however, denouncing the Warsaw rebels as adventurers whose action had upset plans for an orderly advance through Poland. The task of supplying Bor devolved upon a handful of Italian-based British aircraft that parachuted small quantities of supplies into Warsaw at night.

Early in September, either bowing to Anglo-American pressure or confident that the anticommunist Poles were all but wiped out, Stalin at last approved the use of Russian airfields in a supply drop. More than 100 B-17s arrived over Warsaw on 18 September and released almost 1,300 containers of arms, ammunition, food and medical supplies. By this time the perimeter held by Bor's followers had so contracted that accurate parachute delivery was almost impossible. No more than 20 percent of the containers reached the doomed Poles. Apparently Stalin himself refused permission for another attempt to aid the Warsaw insurgents, and early in October the uprising was crushed.

The sporadic Frantic missions had not forced the enemy to divide his forces, as General Arnold had hoped. Fortunately, this failure had no real impact on daylight bombing, for the Mustang had demonstrated its worth even before the shuttle bombing had begun. By using Russian bases, Spaatz extended the range of his bombers to reach synthetic fuel plants, oil refineries and aircraft factories that otherwise could not have been bombed. Whether the attacks on these targets were of major importance remains open to debate; in any event, most of them had fallen to the advancing Red Army before many months.

Anglo-American political leaders had hoped that Frantic would break down the barrier of suspicion that Stalin had erected. Although individual Americans enjoyed the friendship and cooperation of their Russian counterparts, the Soviet dictator made sure that the contagion of foreign ideas did not spread. For example, he imprisoned the officer who had been his chief representative during the Frantic negotiations, Marshal A. A. Novikov, who remained in Siberia until Premier Nikita Khrushchev denounced the crimes of the dead Stalin a decade later.

12. Eyes on Oil

At the outset of the air war against Germany, Royal Air Force Bomber Command tried unsuccessfully to attack the enemy's oil industry. An analysis of aerial photographs revealed the difficulty of hitting even a city by night, let alone as small a target as a refinery or tank farm located within or on the fringe of an urban complex. As a result, oil became just another useless panacea target when Bomber Harris took over the night-bombing effort. He proceeded to direct the Lancasters, Stirlings and Halifaxes against the cities and their inhabitants instead of attacking some specific element of the German economy.

Like Arnold and Eaker, however, Carl Spaatz believed that the American contribution to Operation Pointblank, as the Anglo-American Combined Bomber Offensive was called, should consist of attacks on critical segments of German industry. According to Spaatz, oil production represented the perfect candidate for destruction from the air. It was a vital target, though certainly not an easy one. Oil and gasoline, grease and other lubricants were essential to every weapon in the

Waves of B-24s hit Ploesti in May
1944

enemy arsenal, from Tiger tanks to submarines. Like the manufacture of airplanes or ball bearings, oil refining and synthetic fuel production took place at widely scattered locations, some 80 sites in all, stretching from Ploesti in Rumania diagonally across the continent of Europe to Emmerich, Germany, near the Dutch border. Early in 1944, Allied intelligence estimates indicated that by autumn plants extracting fuel from coal would join crude oil refineries in processing almost 7 million tons of

fuel and lubricants, more than an adequate supply for all of Germany's armed forces.

These estimates, however, told Spaatz that not all the production facilities were of equal importance; 54 of them accounted for 90 percent of the total output, 27 for half of it. Spaatz was confident that during the summer of 1944 the U.S. Strategic Air Forces in Europe—the Eighth and Fifteenth Air Forces—could destroy the 27 plants and with the help

Ploesti refinery after a September 1944 attack

of the British all 54. By September 1944, air power could, he maintained, cut off the enemy's supply of gasoline.

Attacking oil production afforded an opportunity to destroy German aircraft, while at the same time diminishing the amount of fuel available to them. In building synthetic oil plants, the Germans had taken into account the threat of Allied bombing and located them where flak and fighters could provide protection. As a result, the 54 critical targets formed clusters that ensured daylight air battles with Luftwaffe interceptors, actions that would enable the P-51s and P-47s to inflict further punishment on the enemy. The decisive nature of the target and the opportunity to tie down or destroy German aircraft that might otherwise oppose the coming invasion outweighed the probable American losses, for Spaatz believed that his forces were better able than the Luftwaffe to survive battle deaths and downed aircraft.

When Spaatz began formulating this bombing strategy, the invasion of Europe was some months distant. Scheduled for the immediate future were operations to isolate the Normandy beaches and to disrupt transportation throughout the Reich. Eisenhower, Air Chief Marshal Sir Arthur Tedder, who served as the American general's deputy, and Air Chief Marshal Sir Charles Portal, Britain's Chief of Air Staff, agreed that aerial operations in preparation for the assault upon Europe should have priority. Spaatz, though he realized that lines of transportation had to be attacked, wanted something more—permission to throw whatever effort he could spare against oil production.

Bomber Harris did not share Spaatz's enthusiasm for attacking oil processing plants. The British officer doubted that night bombers could conduct precision attacks except against easily located targets such as the Mohne and Eder dams, breached by low-level attack during May 1943. To destroy the oil industry seemed to require daylight precision bombing, a kind of warfare for which Bomber Command was ill suited. Even the Lancaster lacked the ceiling and the defensive armament to survive by day, just as the American Liberators and Flying Fortresses lacked the bomb capacity for city busting and were flown by crews barely acquainted with night flying. Harris understandably wanted to continue operating as he had, specializing in the destruction of industrial cities rather than industrial plants.

Tedder, Spaatz's nominal superior, favored concentrating upon the rail net instead of diluting the effort by attacking petroleum production. Sir Trafford Leigh-Mallory, a sort of officer without portfolio in Eisenhower's headquarters, also opposed the oil offensive. In Washington, General Arnold and Major General Barney M. Giles, who served as Arnold's executive, endorsed the Spaatz strategy but felt the proposal was ill timed. Eisenhower, after all, faced that mighty endeavor, the invasion of Europe, and construction of launch sites for buzz bombs continued, even though these vengeance weapons had not yet begun falling on England.

Significantly, Arnold did not tell his principal commander in Europe to shelve the proposed oil offensive until after the invasion. The commanding general had complete confidence in Spaatz, who had developed a similar relationship with Eisenhower. After agreeing to carry out his share of the campaign against enemy transportation, Spaatz argued the case for using surplus bomber sorties to begin the oil offensive immediately. Legend has it that the airman offered to request reassignment if the Supreme Commander did not accept his judgment in this critical matter. Whether or not Spaatz pressed the issue so vigorously, and he may not have had to, Eisenhower, who had come to value the air officer's opinions, told him to launch the proposed campaign.

Spaatz obtained Arnold's agreement to begin with an attack on the refineries at Ploesti, though the commanding general suggested conducting the raid in conjunction with strikes on nearby railroad marshaling yards. Since the Germans were sending trainloads of men and equipment to oppose the Russian invasion of Rumania, these yards formed an important element in the attempt to disrupt enemy transportation. Three times during April, B-17s and B-24s of the Fifteenth Air Force bombed the Ploesti rail yards, each time inflicting collateral damage upon adjacent refineries that actually were the more important target.

In mid-April, the V-1 threat loomed large, persuading Tedder that Crossbow should take precedence over the oil campaign which Spaatz had just begun. Once again, Eisenhower sided with the American airman, decreeing that the Eighth Air Force should divide its predicted good bombing weather between the two. Before Doolittle could launch a massive strike planned for the petroleum manufacturing centers, cloud descended upon Germany.

Two weeks passed before weather and invasion commitments permitted the Eighth Air Force to join the Fifteenth in attacking the oil industry. On 12 May Doolittle sent 935 bombers, with a formidable es-

Liberator trails smoke after going through heavy
flak

Sequence shows an Me 109 hedgehopping, being
hit, going down in flames

cort, against four synthetic fuel plants clustered about 120 miles southwest of Berlin. Aware how vital these installations had become, the Luftwaffe massed some 200 fighters, shooting down 46 bombers and 10 of the long-range escorts but failing to prevent 90 percent of the raiders from dumping 1,700 tons of explosive on the assigned targets.

Even though D-Day was fast approaching, Spaatz managed to sustain the oil offensive. In eastern Europe, the Fifteenth Air Force attacked Ploesti three times during May and maintained pressure until August, when Russian troops overran the refineries. Meanwhile, the same Royal Air Force group that soon would be parachuting supplies into embattled Warsaw dropped mines in the Danube River to sink oil-laden barges. From the west, Doolittle's bombers attacked again on 28 and 29 May, penetrating as far as Ruhland and Pölitz in eastern Germany.

Albert Speer, the overall director of the German armaments program, recognized the danger posed by systematic attacks on the sources of synthetic fuel. These installations, with their miles of easily fractured pipe, proved especially vulnerable to bomb damage. Doolittle's attacks on 12 May, Speer declared in his memoirs, heralded a "new era in the air war" that ultimately "meant the end of German armaments production." Using both slave and free labor, Speer and his colleagues struggled to maintain production despite continued bombing and the Soviet advance. For example, at Leuna in central Germany, a plant hit hard on 12 and 28 May, the Germans managed to attain 10 percent of capacity in July and almost 30 by November, despite four other air attacks.

Not long after Spaatz began attacking oil production, Bomber Harris agreed to hit 10 plants in the Ruhr Valley in conjunction with attacks on industrial cities. Sometimes he sent a few light twin-engine Mosquito bombers, on other occasions a few hundred Lancasters or Halifaxes. Although willing to cooperate, Harris remained convinced that bombing these installations by night was inherently less efficient than bombing the workers who operated them.

The attacks that Spaatz had launched during April and May, plus the early efforts undertaken by Harris, persuaded Air Commodore S. O. Bufton, Royal Air Force Director of Bombing, to urge that Portal throw the full weight of Bomber Command into the oil offensive. Night attacks had already battered a few synthetic fuel plants; Bufton wanted to destroy oil production throughout the Ruhr, wiping out this portion of a critical industry before the Americans did so.

Once Allied armies had overrun the V-1 sites in the Calais area and liberated much of France, the American and British heavy bombers could return to strategic bombing. Oil targets now headed the priority list for both Bomber Command and Spaatz's American forces. Established in England to help coordinate the campaign was a Joint Oil Targets Committee, which soon decided that the most vulnerable targets were the factories producing synthetic gasoline. As Spaatz had recommended early in the year, the Anglo-American bomber force now attempted to choke off Germany's gasoline supply.

In September, as this combined oil offensive got under way, the Eighth Air Force was recovering from a crisis of morale. Prior to D-Day, Army Air Forces had suspended the policy of transferring individuals to duty in the United States after a specified number of missions, a decision that caused Doolittle's airmen to wonder whether they would have to keep on flying in combat until they were killed. A program of sending men to Atlantic City or some other stateside resort for a brief respite from battle served mainly to kindle resentment against airmen and soldiers who had remained in the United States. By the end of summer, with Allied forces established on the Continent, the rotation policy again went into effect.

As morale improved, the weather deteriorated, giving Speer and his principal deputy, Edmund Geilenberg, a brief respite during which to shift gasoline production from the larger and more vulnerable installations to smaller facilities that used a different process and were harder to locate using H2X. Crude-oil refineries also contributed a trickle of gasoline, for they proved surprisingly resistant to bomb damage. Ironically, Royal Air Force night bombers, employing Oboe or G-H, proved more accurate against these new plants than did the Flying Fortresses or Liberators that had to rely on airborne radar. Weather permitting, the Norden sight still provided the greatest accuracy, but the skies rarely were cloudless, and the defenders emplaced smoke generators around the petroleum production sites.

The ingenuity of Speer and Geilenberg enabled the Luftwaffe from time to time to collect enough fuel to launch hundreds of fighters in defense of the synthetic fuel plants, but the day-to-day protection of these installations rested with the flak batteries. Knowledge that skilled and deadly enemy gunners were waiting weighed heavily upon Doolittle's airmen. When the strain of combat grew too great, the individual was described as "flak happy," a candidate for a "flak home" where he could recuperate from combat fatigue.

At Leuna, for example, antiaircraft fire claimed many a victim. During a 2 November strike by the Eighth Air Force, fragments from bursting shells wounded Second Lieutenant Robert Femoyer, navigator in one of the B-17s. Although bleeding severely and suffering intense pain, he refused an injection of morphine until he had guided the damaged plane safely to the North Sea, evading the many antiaircraft concentrations that barred the way. He died a short time after the Fortress had landed in Britain. He was awarded a posthumous Medal of Honor.

In spite of fighters, flak and persisting overcast, the offensive against the oil industry reached a peak in November, destroying most of the production capacity that Speer and Geilenberg had painstakingly assembled. Doolittle's bombers battered more than 20 plants on 13 days during the month, conducting strikes that varied in severity from the 1,400 tons dropped on Leuna on 2 November to the mere 166 tons that pummeled a small complex at Böhlen on the 30th. The Fifteenth Air Force, hampered by storms over the Alps, landed staggering blows on 10 different days, including a 500-bomber attack against Floridsdorf, Austria, that delivered 1,100 tons of ordnance. Night attacks by Bomber Command, supplemented by an occasional daylight raid, completed the ruin of the 10 Ruhr facilities whose destruction Harris had agreed to undertake. Once this had been accomplished, Portal turned Bomber Command against Pölitz and Leuna, frequent targets of the Eighth Air Force.

Because the Lancaster could carry double the average load of its American counterparts, the British delivered the heavier weight of bombs on a typical mission, 660 tons compared with 388 for Spaatz's aircraft. Speer considered the night raids far more dangerous than daytime strikes, "since heavier bombs are used and an extraordinary accuracy in attacking the target is reported." Thanks to the navigation and bombing aids devised by British science, Bomber Command had struck with greater precision than Harris had anticipated.

The Allied offensive bore down heaviest upon the suppliers of aviation gasoline, though the Germans managed to gather enough for an occasional foray. The unsuccessful Ardennes counterthrust depended, for example, upon stockpiles that Speer had collected, and this action not only consumed aviation gasoline to no lasting advantage but also devoured diesel fuel, lubricants and low-octane gasoline for vehicles. In the meantime, the Russian advance both swallowed up the Rumanian and Polish refineries and forced the Germans to squander every type of petroleum product in the vain effort to halt the Red Army.

The oil offensive had important side effects that not even Spaatz had foreseen. Nitrogen formerly produced at the burned-out synthetic fuel plants had been essential for the manufacture of synthetic rubber, explosives and fertilizer. By bombing these installations, the Allies had disrupted the entire German chemical industry, affecting everyone from farmer to front-line soldier.

As the year 1945 began, Speer realized that he could do no more. Oil production would never recover from the effects of the Anglo-American bombing. Aerial bombardment had crippled an essential element of the German war machine.

Time off: Bomber crew spends a
quiet evening at home

Near miss: Falling bombs by chance almost hit FW 190

13. From the Ashes

The appearance of American Mustangs and Thunderbolts over Berlin may have convinced Hermann Göring that Germany could not win the war, as he told General Spaatz after the fighting had ended, but Albert Speer saw these long-range fighters, and the bombers they escorted, as another challenge to his administrative skill. Concluding that Germany had to have fighters to meet the daylight threat, he established the *Jägerstab*, or Fighter Committee, headed by Karl Saur. This agency of Speer's Ministry of Armaments and War Production took charge of dispersing fighter assembly plants and increasing output.

Not even the support of Speer, suave courtier and masterly bureaucrat, could enable Saur to obtain a completely free hand in building fighters. Adolf Hitler took a personal interest in aircraft manufacture, and he was obsessed with the construction of bombers so that the Luftwaffe might return to the attack. Not until the summer of 1944, some four months after Doolittle's bombers and their escorting fighters had

133

tested the defenses of Berlin, did the chief of the Fighter Committee obtain first priority for his product.

The German dictator had scarcely made this decision when he changed his mind. Early in August, he summoned Speer and Galland, the fighter commander, to his headquarters, where the two men learned that the Führer planned to send the reconstituted Luftwaffe into combat in support of ground forces in France, rather than using it against the bomber offensive. The production minister and the airman both suggested that such a decision would result in the collapse of the armaments program under a deluge of bombs, but as they spoke, they could see that Hitler, who had recently survived an assassination attempt, was becoming nervous and angry. Speer recalled that the leader's "expression, . . . the lively fluttering of his hands, the way he chewed his fingernails" indicated that "he was growing increasingly tense." Finally, Hitler lost control of his emotions, shouting that operational matters were none of Speer's business and ordering the two subordinates out of the room.

On the following day, Hitler summoned Galland and Speer into his presence. "This time," the armaments minister wrote in his memoirs, "Hitler's rage was even more violent; he spoke faster and faster, stumbling over his own words." The Führer told Galland to disband the fighter arm and Speer to cease all aircraft production. The skilled workers were to be reemployed in turning out antiaircraft guns, a task for which they were singularly ill-suited. Used to his leader's tantrums, Speer expected him to allow this policy, adopted in anger, to expire when calm returned, but Hitler instead issued a formal directive terminating fighter production. "That was the first command from Hitler," Speer later declared, "that neither Saur nor I obeyed." They ordered that the building of fighters continue, and a few days later the German dictator did, indeed, change his mind, reassigning the highest priority to fighter construction.

Despite Hitler's meddling, Saur was able to frustrate Allied attempts to cripple the aircraft industry. He took a group of factories operating at far less than capacity, dispersed their operations to reduce vulnerability to bombing, placed them on a wartime footing and turned out thousands of planes instead of the hundreds that had been built a few years earlier. Thanks in part to slave labor, production soared from 1,300 in January 1944 to almost 3,000 in September of that year, and the monthly average hovered between 2,300 and 2,700 through December.

Fortresses blast an aircraft plant at Wiener
Neustadt, near Vienna

Single-engine fighter production for 1944 increased by 300 percent over the previous year, acceptances of twin-engine fighters were 50 percent greater, and in addition Saur diverted many new twin-engine bombers to the night fighter force.

The bulk of the single-engine fighters were advanced models of the Me 109 and FW 190, most of which battled the daytime raiders, though some fought at night as Wild Boars. Luftwaffe pilots devised new tactics for the day fighters they were receiving. Radar controllers on the ground would track the American bombers and the fighter escort, reporting the location of the protective screen and advising of any gaps in the column of bombardment wings. Instead of predictably attacking from the front in pairs or groups of four, the Germans now sometimes accepted the risk of collision and massed ahead of the bombers, presenting more fast-approaching targets than the nose and chin turrets could handle. At other times the Germans struck two or four at a time from both front and rear, particularly effective tactics when radar controllers discovered a break in the seemingly endless succession of combat formations.

By the middle of 1944, Messerschmitt engineers were squeezing the last bit of performance out of the fighter that had first rolled from the Bayerische Flugzeugwerke almost a decade before. Known at the time as the Bf 109, the aircraft had proved so effective that the German Air Ministry canceled production of an even better fighter, Ernst Heinkel's He 100D, after a total run of just 13 aircraft. The basis for this decision was the assumption that the war would be too short to justify the manufacture of two similar types. Now, as the fifth year of combat drew to a close, several plans were under consideration to extend the life of the Me 109.

Entering production were the Me 109H and K, high-altitude versions with an enlarged wing and, in some models, a pressurized cabin. The Ks featured a Daimler-Benz engine fitted with a nitrous oxide or methanol injection device to boost power in emergencies. Some of these high-flying airplanes served as reconnaissance craft.

A series of attempts to build a fighter loosely based on the Me 209, originally a racing version of the Me 109, petered out during 1944. In the hands of test pilot Fritz Wendel, the Me 209V-5 had demonstrated its superiority to the Me 109Gs then in quantity production. Cleaner, faster and more powerful than the standard Messerschmitt, the prototype could claw its way above 42,000 feet and attain speeds approaching 500 miles per hour. But Speer and Saur did not dare suspend Me 109 production to retool for a different, even though potentially better, fighter.

For more than a year, Richard Vogt of the Blohm and Voss seaplane firm had been trying to create a high-altitude fighter by attaching a huge wing to the modified fuselage of an Me 109. The hybrid's wing span measured 67 feet, with two radiators mounted midway between root and tip. Although a test model, the BV 155V2, reached an altitude of 56,000 feet, the craft never entered production.

Many more changes remained to be rung on Kurt Tank's FW 190, which during its varied career did everything from intercept bombers to drop aerial torpedoes. The FW 190D, powered by a Junkers liquid-cooled engine instead of the usual Bavarian Motor Works radial, proved a deadly interceptor. This airplane retained the aerodynamically clean lines of the series, even though the fuselage had to be lengthened to accommodate the new engine. Thanks to methanol-and-water injection, which boosted output by more than 25 percent, the Junkers power plant could produce 2,240 horsepower in an emergency.

The deadly and handsome FW 190D so impressed the German Air Ministry that Tank received permission to use his own prefix, "Ta," instead of "FW" (for "Focke-Wulf,") on planes that his team designed for the company. His first effort was the Ta 152, an improved FW 190D, capable of 472 miles per hour, using methanol boost, at about 41,000 feet. Some 600 of these fighters had rolled from the assembly line when Germany surrendered.

Among the more spectacular designs to emerge from German drawing boards during World War II was Claude Dornier's Do 335 *Pfeil* (Arrow). Based on a tractor-pusher design that Dornier had patented in 1937, the experimental version took to the air in 1943, powered by two 1,800-horsepower Daimler-Benz engines. One of them, mounted in the conventional location ahead of the pilot, pulled the craft along, while the second, buried in the fuselage behind the cockpit, turned a pusher propeller mounted aft of the cruciform tail surfaces. Unlike the arrow, for which it was named, the plane tended to porpoise at high speed, unless the pilot had a deft touch on the controls. Dornier had delivered just a handful of the planes when the war ended.

On 28 July 1944, three stubby German fighters, painted in a rust-colored camouflage pattern, dived on an American bomber formation near Merseberg. When the Mustang escort tried to intervene, the enemy scattered, diving away at speeds the P-51s could not equal. As

137

one of the Mustang pilots later reported, "I had no time to get my sights anywhere near them."

One day later, Captain Arthur Jeffrey, flying a P-38, spotted one of these new German aircraft streaking toward the formation he was protecting. Jeffrey and his wingman chased the intruder through a rapid succession of climbs and dives. The captain scored hits on the enemy plane, which released puffs of smoke before disappearing beneath an overcast. As he pulled up at an indicated air speed of 500 miles per hour, Jeffrey blacked out momentarily but regained consciousness and returned safely to England. An examination of the film in his gun camera convinced Eighth Air Force intelligence officers that he had scored a kill, but his intended victim actually escaped.

This new kind of enemy aircraft, which lacked both a propeller and a conventional horizontal stabilizer, was the Me 163 *Komet,* propelled

Me 109s on the assembly line at Wiener Neustadt factory

Mustang peels off during a bomber escort mission

by a Walter rocket engine. In 1938 Alexander Lippisch had designed a tailless glider for testing small rocket engines, but within three years a strengthened model was attaining speeds in excess of 600 miles per hour, when the rocket was ignited after the tow plane had cut loose the streamlined craft. Lippisch set to work in December 1941 to convert the experimental glider into a fighter, retaining the teardrop shape and swept-back wing of the original.

The *Komet* proved deadly in combat and dangerous to fly. In one case, for instance, three Me 163s attacking in single file at 600 miles per hour downed three Mustangs with cannon fire in just one pass. On the other hand, the Walter engine was inherently hazardous. Pilots took off under rocket power with fuel enough for no more than 12 minutes of combustion. They burned this in brief bursts before gliding to a landing, and American airmen reported seeing large smoke rings whenever the *Komet* rocket ignited. Anyone who brought one of the Me 163s in for a landing with hydrazine hydrate and methyl alcohol still in the tanks risked an explosion. Several pilots died in this type of accident.

More promising than the rocket-powered interceptor was the jet fighter. In August 1939, shortly before Hitler's invasion of Poland, the Heinkel factory tested its model 178, a shoulder-wing monoplane powered by a turbine engine. Although difficult to handle and plagued by a faulty retractable landing gear, the He 178 demonstrated the feasibility of jet propulsion and provided data for future designs.

Indeed, Robert Lusser, a designer for the Heinkel firm, soon turned his attention to the jet fighter, producing the twin-turbine He 280. This craft had a maximum endurance of 45 minutes and featured an ejection seat powered by compressed air to hurl the pilot clear if the plane became crippled. Its great effectiveness in mock combat against an FW 190 during 1943 persuaded Ernst Heinkel, though not the Air Ministry, of the superiority of the jet fighter. But because of official indifference, the He 280 reverted to experimental status.

In little more than a year, however, Anglo-American bombing had convinced these same policy makers that Germany had to have not just a new jet fighter but one that could be assembled by unskilled workers at factories scattered throughout the Reich, using a minimum of scarce metals. On the strength of a crude mock-up, Heinkel received a contract, then turned out a prototype in just 65 days. When it rolled from a factory near Vienna, the He 162 featured a bonded wooden skin over an aluminum skeleton. A single jet engine sat atop the fuselage behind the cockpit.

This Heinkel product, nicknamed the *Volksjäger*, or people's fighter, proved ill-starred from the outset. On its first flight, an undercarriage door tore free, and during a formal demonstration for Nazi officials, the plywood leading edge separated from one wing, followed by wing tip and aileron, as the test aircraft broke up and crashed. This accident and incidents in subsequent flights by other models prompted the company's designers to increase the size of the twin vertical stabilizers, move the center of gravity forward by placing lead above the nose wheel, and add down-turned wing tips. After these modifications, the *Volksjäger* flew well enough, though the turbine engine consumed fuel at a rate that would have limited combat missions to about 20 minutes. No missions were flown, however, for the fighter had just begun reaching combat units when the war ended.

Although Heinkel had pioneered in jet aviation, Messerschmitt produced the world's first operational jet fighter. Initial planning had begun shortly after the He 178 flew successfully, but the Air Ministry assigned such a low priority to the Messerschmitt effort that jet-powered flights did not begin until July 1942. The company engineers placed two Junkers turbine engines beneath the wing but chose an ordinary dual landing gear which so raised the sharklike nose that the pilot could barely see to taxi or take off. Substitution of a tricycle landing gear solved this problem.

The untried turbine engines caused the Luftwaffe many an uneasy moment. Besides providing dazzling speed, the new power plants did not require high-test gasoline, an important advantage after Spaatz launched his oil offensive during 1944. But they consumed cruder fuel at a rapid rate, though the Me 262 carried enough to cruise for 90 minutes in the substratosphere. Fast maneuvering or extended flight in dense air at low altitude, however, cut sharply into the plane's supply. The first two engines mated to the prototype failed while being run up prior to the scheduled first flight and had to be replaced. Engine reliability remained a problem throughout the program, with frequent overhaul necessary. Usually this work devolved upon men who had little experience with these revolutionary power plants.

Curtis LeMay and his Regensburg strike force inadvertently dealt the program a setback on 17 August 1943, destroying tools that were slated for use in manufacturing jet fighters. This difficulty proved trifling, however, compared with the disruptions that stemmed from the indecision or outright meddling of Adolf Hitler. According to Speer, Hitler postponed a decision on Me 262 production, thus forcing the program to limp along until January 1944, when he told the armaments minister that he wanted "as many aircraft of this type as we could make in the shortest possible time." Speer was shocked, however, at the Führer's insistence that all the Me 262s be used as bombers. If necessary, they were to be stripped of their four 30-mm cannon to boost ordnance capacity to half a ton.

P-51 bears in on a jet-powered Me 262

January 1945: B-17 readies for a snowy takeoff

Production, Speer believed, would amount to 50 planes a month during the last half of 1944 and 210 each month beginning in January 1945. These estimates proved wildly optimistic, partly because Anglo-American bombing had a hand in the matter. The thousands of excellent conventionally powered fighters manufactured under Saur's guidance languished for lack of gasoline and could not give the jet factories the protection these critical installations deserved. Nor could replacement pilots receive adequate flight training in a fuel-starved Reich.

Despite the lagging rate of Me 262 production, Galland ignored Hitler's policy and in the fall of 1944 formed an experimental jet fighter unit, initially equipped with 30 of the scarce aircraft. The commander was Walter Nowotny, who had already received credit for more than 250 aerial victories. During six weeks, in spite of recurring engine trouble, this small force of jets destroyed as many as 26 American aircraft, though

143

it lost almost the same number. Among the Me 262 pilots killed was Nowotny himself. The vast majority of German casualties resulted from accidents, for airmen were entering combat after as few as 10 hours in the complicated jet fighter.

One of the Me 262 pilots, Heinz Bär, downed five Americans to become history's first jet fighter ace and increase his wartime total to 220 aircraft. Galland, disillusioned by the petty bickering within the high command and out of favor with Hitler, took personal command of one of the new jet units as the war was ending. In the hands of veterans like Nowotny, Bär and Galland, the Me 262 was a deadly weapon; rarely, however, could the Luftwaffe muster more than 50 of the planes, and the number engaged in any one action seldom exceeded a dozen.

Piecemeal introduction of the jet interceptor gave the Allies an opportunity to locate the production centers and attack them, with bombers diverted from oil or transportation targets. In January 1945, for example, Spaatz decided that crippling jet production constituted what the Army Air Forces official history described as a "parallel obligation," on a par with the oil offensive. Despite resourceful production methods, a supply of forced labor for the more menial jobs, and brilliant designs, the German aircraft industry succumbed, as much a victim of the country's political leadership as it was of Allied air power. When Hitler in March 1945 decided to commit the entire jet program to fighter production, the phoenix that Speer and Saur had coaxed from the ashes had again been consumed by fire.

14. Thunderclap and Clarion

The oil offensive, decisive though it proved, did not absorb the entire energies of the Anglo-American bomber force. Emergencies arose from time to time to attract bombs that might otherwise have demolished refineries and synthetic fuel plants. Reports that tanks were rolling from assembly lines and moving immediately eastward to oppose Soviet armor caused a diversion of the bombing effort, as did the appearance of the jet fighter. In addition, others besides Spaatz had recommendations for shortening the war by using the strategic bomber in some specific manner.

During September 1944, with the Allied armies established in Europe, General Eisenhower released control of the Anglo-American heavy bombers. No longer did Sir Charles Portal direct the Combined Bomber Offensive, an assignment he had carried out from the Casablanca conference at the beginning of 1943 until Eisenhower had taken over in preparation for D-Day. Now Portal, acting through his Deputy Chief of Air Staff, Air Marshal Sir Norman Bottomley, shared responsi-

145

B-17s and B-24s meet high over Germany in
early 1945

bility with General Arnold, who allowed Spaatz almost a free hand in the day-to-day operation of the American strategic air forces in Europe. The change acknowledged the increased importance of the Eighth and Fifteenth Air Forces, which now ranged from the Danube to the Rhine, a revolutionary change since January 1943, when Eaker's bombers were merely hacking at the perimeter of Hitler's Europe.

Portal, though he endorsed the oil offensive, also believed that a brief but savage attack upon Berlin by every heavy bomber available to the Allies might yet knock Germany out of the war. As early as August 1944, he suggested preparing for such an operation, called Thunderclap, but his own staff remained cool toward the idea, believing that its time had not yet come.

Although Bomber Harris was participating in the oil offensive, the area bombing of industrial cities remained his primary objective. He opposed tying the bombing campaign to any specific type of target, mainly because he resented the restrictions imposed on Bomber Command by "outsiders"—even though that outsider might be the Chief of Air Staff, or his deputy, or even Sir Arthur Tedder, deputy to General Eisenhower. Indeed, the only outsider with whom Harris worked in harmony was Eisenhower himself, when the Supreme Commander took charge of the heavy bombers during the spring and summer of 1944.

In justifying his objections to attacking categories of related targets, Harris insisted that the ability to hit towns more or less at random kept the enemy off balance and reduced British casualties, an argument he continued to use after the German fighter force had run so short of fuel that his bombers could attack day or night. As for Thunderclap, he seemed to believe that this special operation could accomplish nothing that normal area attacks could not do.

Another suggestion came from Tedder, who complained that the Combined Bomber Offensive, which should form "one comprehensive pattern," actually resembled "a patchwork quilt." In suggesting a type of target that would unify the strategic bombing campaign, he said that the "one common factor in the whole German war effort from the political control down to the supply of troops in the front line is communications." As a result, roads, railways, canals and marshaling yards should become prime targets, though the oil campaign would continue in order to cut off the supply of diesel fuel and gasoline necessary for highway traffic.

Portal had consistently opposed this kind of undertaking for fear that the heavy bombers would end up attacking small targets scattered all across Germany. Tedder believed, however, that comparatively few attacks by strategic bombers, most of them delivered in the Ruhr and Rhineland, "could rapidly produce a state of chaos" that would weaken not only the defenses barring the Allied advance into Germany but the entire enemy war machine. The British Air Staff showed little enthusiasm for this proposal, since it seemed likely to compete with the oil offensive, even though Tedder had included oil refineries and synthetic fuel plants among the transportation targets.

To help decide among rival strategies and to assess the various emergencies that arose to threaten the ground or air offensives, the Allies established a Combined Strategic Targets Committee. Here British and American military officers, political scientists and economists reviewed intelligence concerning the state of the various target systems that either were being bombed or might require air attack. A series of subcommittees dealt with such categories as German oil production (which had formerly been the specialty of the Joint Oil Targets Committee), aircraft manufacture, tank production and communications.

The subcommittee on communications at first offered Tedder no encouragement for the kind of air offensive he was proposing. He did, however, obtain powerful support from members of Eisenhower's staff. Among Tedder's partisans was Professor Solly Zuckerman, who had analyzed the effect of attacks on transportation during the early phases of the Italian campaign. This study had convinced Zuckerman that the key targets in attacking communications were rail centers, where marshaling yards held large numbers of locomotives and boxcars, war material filled vulnerable warehouses and rolling stock was built or repaired. This so-called Zuckerman thesis, together with the successful bombing of French railways before D-Day, provided strong, though occasionally contradictory, evidence in support of Tedder. The principal contradiction arose from Zuckerman's insistence that roads and individual bridges were not worth attacking, whereas the destruction of the Seine bridges had immobilized the road-bound German divisions poised north of Paris. Of course, Tedder was thinking exclusively in terms of heavy bombers, and flak-protected bridges seemed difficult and unprofitable targets for either high-flying B-17s or Lancasters attacking by night.

With Tedder presenting a logical case for bombing the centers of communication and Spaatz pointing out the increasing impact of the oil offensive, Allied planners compromised. Hopeful of winning the war in

With one engine aflame, a Fortress goes
down over Berlin

1944, the major commanders met late in October at Eisenhower's headquarters and agreed that oil should retain the top priority, while second place went to land and water communications throughout the rapidly contracting Thousand-Year Reich. The arrangement satisfied both Spaatz and Tedder, and early in November American strategic bombers went into action against the German rail system.

The assignment of transportation targets caught the Eighth Air Force staff off balance, but the members quickly gathered the necessary photos, maps and other data needed to plan missions against railyards and repair facilities at towns like Bielefeld, Cologne, Coblenz, Hamm, Hamburg, Frankfurt and Ludwigshafen. Since oil continued to take precedence, these strikes had to be scheduled among raids on Leuna, Gelsenkirchen and other places where synthetic fuel was produced.

Joining the Eighth Air Force in American contribution to the Anglo-American transportation campaign was the Fifteenth Air Force, which bored through clouds to cross the Alps and hit rail targets in Austria and southern Germany, and also pounded similar objectives in Hungary. RAF Bomber Command planted mines in the Danube but threw most of its weight against western Germany. Among the most successful attacks was a British raid that cut the Dortmund-Ems canal near Ladbergen, damaging it so extensively that it remained closed for the remainder of the year.

As these attacks began, the Combined Strategic Target Committee completed work on a formal plan for systematically attacking German communications in nine specific areas. These targets lay as far east as Breslau and Vienna, but most were clustered along the Rhine River and the Dortmund-Ems canal. The selection of target groupings for intensive attack would depend upon the military situation, east and west.

At the end of November, after the transportation network had borne second priority for a month, Eisenhower's intelligence analysts reviewed the results thus far. They concluded that Germany was hard pressed for experienced trainmen, locomotives and freight cars, shortages caused at least in part by the aerial offensive against enemy communications. This condition was a handicap, however, rather than a total disability, for the trains and barges kept moving; weapons, ammunition and food continued to reach the battlefronts. Success seemed to be eluding the Allied strategic bombers, even though they were dropping a greater weight of explosives upon the transportation routes than upon the oil industry.

The German counteroffensive, launched from the cover of the Ardennes in mid-December, triggered a savage Allied bombing of communications arteries throughout western Germany, as the Anglo-American air power sought to isolate the Bulge battlefield. In this torrent of bombs, the distinction between strategic and tactical operations temporarily vanished. During the last half of December, for example, the Eighth Air Force dropped some 23,000 tons of bombs, 95 percent of them directed against German communications, especially the routes sustaining the enemy thrust. Once again the bombing proved hard to evaluate, but Albert Speer later conceded that strikes against marshaling yards, choke points along rail lines and bridges, whether delivered by fighters or heavy bombers, had proved decisive in containing the German breakthrough.

Early in January 1945, after the Battle of the Bulge was over, Allied military leaders again reviewed the air strategy they had adopted for the European theater. In effect, Spaatz, Bottomley and their colleagues decided on more of the same. They reaffirmed that attacks on oil production had first priority, though the bombing of jet aircraft plants was judged equally important. Transportation targets retained second place, with special emphasis now placed upon isolating the Ruhr. This heavily bombed manufacturing and coal-producing region became critical to German survival after Soviet troops overran Silesia, depriving the Reich of that region's coal deposits.

Heavy bombers proved successful in isolating the Ruhr. Methodical attacks began in mid-February, after canals and the three main rail lines had already sustained grave damage. Bomber Command could operate day or night with losses that Harris considered trifling compared with those his crews had endured a year earlier. So overwhelming was Allied air supremacy that key railroad bridges could be singled out for attack, like the Bielefeld viaduct, damaged on 22 February 1945, hit several times by American B-24s, and then totally destroyed in mid-March by 22,000-pound bombs dropped from Lancasters through a late afternoon haze. After the war, American investigators found convincing evidence that aerial bombing had halted the movement of coal from the Ruhr to the rest of Germany. Although the amount of coal taken from the ground declined steadily, stockpiles at the mines soared from a normal 415,000 tons in August 1944 to 2.75 million tons in February. As the noose tightened about the Ruhr, the contents of the storage bunkers swelled to three times the usual seasonal level.

Attack on Hamburg leaves remains of prefabri-
cated U-boat sections

The disruption of German transportation was not confined to the Ruhr. Areas nominated by the Combined Strategic Targets Committee came under attack throughout the Reich. The Fifteenth Air Force, for instance, lavished bombs upon the Vienna railyards as Soviet troops approached the city. The Eighth Air Force also attempted to hamper the movement of German soldiers and equipment in the face of the Russian advance by attacking Chemnitz, Magdeburg and Dresden on the same day, 14 February 1945.

By the time of the raids on these three cities, the transportation offensive had become intertwined with the Thunderclap plan, originally considered during the late summer of 1944 but quietly shelved. The revival of Thunderclap began in January 1945 when Sir Norman Bottomley, Portal's deputy, suggested that the destruction of Berlin, while the Red Army continued its attack, would create "the appearance of close co-ordination in planning between the Russians and ourselves" and strike a damaging blow to German morale. From this seed grew the notion of bombing Berlin or some other town in eastern Germany to assist the Soviet offensive. Besides undermining the German will to resist, this kind of aerial attack would trigger the exodus of tens of thousands of refugees to swell the ranks of the hundreds of thousands already fleeing the Russians. The mass migration of homeless and destitute persons would further tax the capacity not only of the German transportation net but also of relief agencies and other administrative services.

During preparations for the Anglo-American military talks at Malta in January 1945 and the conference of Allied leaders at Yalta in the Crimea during February, the revived Thunderclap plan received consideration. After Churchill had shown interest in using bombers to harry the Germans retreating on the eastern front, Portal suggested "one big attack on Berlin," the basic Thunderclap operation, "and attacks on Dresden, Leipzig, Chemnitz, or any other cities where a severe blitz will not only cause confusion in the evacuation from the East but will also hamper the movement of troops from the West." Eager to have some plan of action available by the time he met Stalin at Yalta, the Prime Minister endorsed the idea.

On the eve of the meeting at Malta, Bottomley conferred with Spaatz, working out a tentative agreement that reaffirmed the precedence given the oil offensive but assigned the Eighth Air Force and Bomber Command a secondary task of bombing Berlin and other east German cities whose destruction would hamper enemy troop movements. Spaatz, in fact, told Bottomley that he already had set in motion an Eighth Air Force raid on Berlin, which was carried out on 3 February. During the Malta conversations, Major General Laurence Kuter, representing the ill General Arnold, endorsed the proposed attacks on communication hubs in eastern Germany.

At Yalta, the plan apparently escaped formal consideration by the Anglo-American Combined Chiefs of Staff, who did not present it to the Russians. The Red Army Chief of Staff did, however, submit a memorandum listing various ways the British and Americans could aid the Soviet offensive. Although these proposals included attacks on transportation centers, specifically Berlin and Leipzig, the Russian seemed more concerned that bombing east of a Berlin-Dresden-Vienna line might interfere with operations by his own forces. Kuter then pointed out that such a line would prevent further attacks on oil plants at Ruhland and Pölitz and also spare transportation centers near Berlin and Dresden, even though these cities and Vienna, as well, would remain subject to air attack. On this note, the discussion ended. The Portal plan was not formally considered, nor did the conferees agree upon a bomb line in eastern Europe. The tabling of the Russian memorandum, however, was interpreted as an endorsement of the kind of raids that Portal had suggested to Churchill. As a result, the way was clear for the destruction not only of Berlin and Leipzig, which the Soviet talking paper had mentioned by name, but of Dresden and other cities that had thus far avoided massive attack.

Doubts already were stirring in Washington about the ethical implications of these raids. The 3 February strike against Berlin's Tempelhof railyards pitted 1,003 American bombers against the flak defenses of the battered capital. In spite of a cloudless sky that permitted use of the Norden sight, the bombing proved inaccurate, owing in part to low-hanging smoke, and much of the 2,265 tons of bombs exploded in residential areas. Both German propagandists and neutral nationals reported that civilian casualties were numerous.

Propaganda broadcasts claiming that between 20,000 and 25,000 noncombatants had perished in an American terror bombing of Berlin upset the Army Air Forces leadership. From Yalta, where the conference was in progress, Kuter asked Spaatz whether the recent decision to bomb Berlin and other transportation targets in eastern Germany, a policy that Kuter himself had reviewed at Malta, was degenerating into indiscriminate attacks on cities. From Washington, General Barney Giles

Ruins of the German Foreign Ministry after
Berlin bombings

echoed this question. Spaatz assured them, however, that the Eighth
and Fifteenth Air Forces were bombing transportation facilities that
had obvious military value but happened to lie within cities. The attacks, he added, were being delivered at the request of the Russians and
seemed to be helping the Red Army's advance. Berlin, in fact, was one
of the two cities specifically mentioned in the memorandum submitted
by the Soviet delegates at Yalta.

Other justifiable targets lay within Dresden, which had scarcely
been damaged by the one previous air attack it had endured. To Spaatz,
the city represented an appendage to several military objectives, among
them a cluster of small manufacturing plants, nearby army bases and the
marshaling yard. To Bomber Harris, it was just another enemy city deserving of destruction. To tens of thousands of noncombatants fleeing a

Soviet army just 40 miles away, Dresden offered a place of refuge, a haven that was to become a trap.

Not only was Dresden crowded with more refugees than local authorities could care for, it was almost defenseless. The night barrier constructed by Josef Kammhuber now lay in ruins. The key radar sites had been overrun by Eisenhower's forces, and fuel for the night fighters was carefully rationed. Flak defenses were weak, and the surviving German day fighters, including 50 or so jets, had massed in the Hamburg area, husbanding fuel for an occasional foray against American bombers.

On the night of 13–14 February, Harris dispatched two attacks against Dresden, scheduled about three hours apart, plus a diversionary effort to trick the night fighters into consuming their gasoline before the raiders arrived. These tactics worked to perfection. Very shortly the city was turned into a huge funeral pyre. On the following day the Eighth Air Force arrived, depositing 771 tons of high-explosive and incendiary bombs on the already devastated city. Another American formation

pounded the smoking ruins on 15 February, dropping more than 400 tons of explosives and raising the number of inhabitants killed to perhaps 35,000.

The two Eighth Air Force attacks on Dresden, plus the 14 February raids against Chemnitz and Magdeburg, inspired press stories that the U.S. Strategic Air Forces in Europe had embarked upon a campaign of terror bombing designed to shatter German resistance. General Arnold, who had resumed his duties, inquired whether Spaatz had indeed adopted such a policy and received assurance that the Eighth and Fifteenth Air Forces bombed only military targets. In actual effect, however, the difference between bombing targets with military value, as was the aim under Spaatz, and city busting, as practiced by Bomber Command under Harris, was often more apparent than real.

Unless in the hands of a highly skilled operator, the H2X radar presented an image that resulted in accuracy comparable with that achieved by nighttime area strikes. And even in good weather, targets became

harder to find. As the war neared its end, the Americans were bombing cities that already lay in ruins, with familiar aiming points obliterated, factories reduced to shells and production relocated to scattered sites. With hundreds of Flying Fortresses or Liberators hitting one of Speer's new style synthetic fuel plants or even a railroad marshaling yard, bombs inevitably missed the mark, whether the attackers used H2X or the Norden sight.

The numbers of bombers and the volume of explosives dropped frequently resulted in unnecessary devastation, which was certainly the case at Dresden. Moreover, destruction invited further destruction. Participants in at least one of the final missions of the war said that briefing officers acknowledged the ruin already caused by simply instructing the crews to aim for the center of a built-up area, since the individual targets had already been leveled.

Self-preservation also affected accuracy. A veteran aircrew member, for example, once looked through the plexiglas nose and realized that his bomber and all the others in sight were veering ever so slightly from course, maintaining their alignment as they flinched from the antiaircraft shells bursting ahead of them.

Although these factors conspired against precision, the U.S. Strategic Air Forces in Europe almost always directed its efforts against specific military targets. On only one occasion did the Eighth Air Force take part in an operation designed to overawe the German people with a demonstration of aerial might. In January 1945, Robert Lovett, Assistant Secretary of War for Air, approached General Arnold with a proposal to send swarms of fighter-bombers over Germany, attacking everything from railroad crossings to canal barges and bringing the war to towns that had not yet seen an Allied aircraft.

This one-day attack, which Lovett called the Jeb Stuart operation in honor of the fast-striking Confederate cavalry leader, became Operation Clarion, in which both heavy bombers and fighters would participate. Since Clarion involved attacks on places not yet subjected to air strikes, many a target would be defenseless. Hence the risk to the big bombers would be minimal.

159

Extending the air war in this fashion troubled Ira Eaker, who raised the question of terror bombing. Employing his considerable rhetorical skill, he argued against Clarion on the grounds that "we should never allow the history of this war to convict us of throwing the strategic bomber at the man in the street." The Combined Strategic Targets Committee took the pragmatic view that Clarion would not prove worth the massive effort. Spaatz decided, nevertheless, to launch the operation as soon as clear weather exposed Germany to simultaneous attack.

The weather seemed adequate, though not perfect, on 22 February for the 1,411 Eighth Air Force bombers that ranged Germany in small groups, attacking from altitudes of about 10,000 feet to improve accuracy. Despite this precaution, some of the planes accidentally hit Schaffhausen, Switzerland, for the second time during the war. The Fifteenth Air Force attacked in the east, and Bomber Command battered the Ruhr, as part of the campaign to cut off Germany's coal supply. Although Spaatz was sufficiently impressed to repeat Clarion on the following day, German morale showed no abrupt decline, and rail movement did not come to a sudden halt.

Although Clarion accomplished less than Spaatz had hoped, the attack on transportation proved successful. The fuel shortage choked off road traffic, bombing isolated the Ruhr and the attacks on Dresden and other eastern cities prevented either reinforcement or orderly retreat. On 7 April Portal concluded that further area bombing of German cities would only serve to complicate the task of the occupying armies and called off these raids. Although heavy bombers continued to fly missions in support of the ground forces, the last American strategic bombing occurred on 10 April, when Doolittle sent 1,232 B-17s and B-24s against Berlin.

On 16 April, Spaatz formally announced the end of the daylight bombing offensive in a message to Doolittle and to Twining, the Fifteenth Air Force commander. "The advances of our ground forces," he told his two principal subordinates, "have brought to a close the strategic air war waged by the United States Strategic Air Forces and the Royal Air Force Bomber Command." The air war, he continued, had "been won with a decisiveness becoming increasingly evident as our armies overrun Germany." He then extended his congratulations for past accomplishments and urged all units "to continue with undiminished effort and precision the final tactical phase of air action to secure the ultimate objective—complete defeat of Germany."

The daylight strategic bombing campaign launched by Eaker against the Sotteville marshaling yard on 17 August 1943 had come to an end. Three weeks of tactical operations remained before Germany surrendered. Hitler's Reich, hamstrung by the bombing of oil production and transportation centers, had been torn to pieces by ground armies.

Eighth Air Force pilot Lieutenant Colonel
Walker Mahurin had 21 victories

15. The Balance Sheet

The story of the Eighth Air Force is a saga of human courage—the triumph of determination, discipline and group loyalty over the individual's instinct for survival. The officers and men of the air crews shared danger and discomfort. Together they endured the cold and faced death, continually reassessing their chances of completing the number of missions—which was subject to change—that would assure automatic reassignment to the United States. This routine courage, this pitting of will against emotion, went almost unnoticed, since so many men exhibited it. Late in the war, on a single morning, 10,000 crewmen might don heavy flight suits over their fatigues, take a quick look at their parachutes, then spend the better part of the day breathing oxygen as their bombers bored through the substratosphere. For these men, existence seemed unworldly, with contrails by the thousands gleaming in the sunlight, the earth sometimes disappearing beneath a purplish haze, and bearlike creatures sharing their aircraft. For any individual, life might end abruptly in a fireball or slowly as his blood drained away.

On this battleground, a total of 17 persons, all of them members of bomber crews, earned the Medal of Honor while serving in the Eighth Air Force. They were officers and enlisted men, professionals and wartime soldiers, and they performed every duty that a crew member might be assigned.

The first person so honored was a bombardier, First Lieutenant Jack W. Mathis, who sustained mortal wounds from a flak burst during an 18 March 1943 mission against Vegesack, Germany. Serving as lead bombardier, he was just seconds from the release point when the exploding shell hurled him to the rear of his compartment, but he crawled back to his post, manned the Norden sight and placed his bombs squarely on target. Ironically, Mathis was the only member of this crew to die during 59 missions over Europe.

Pilots or copilots received the greatest number of these awards, and included in this category was First Lieutenant Edward Michael. Although badly wounded by cannon fire from attacking fighters, Michael brought his damaged B-17G out of a flat spin. Since the incendiary bombs on board had begun igniting, he ordered the crew to bail out, only to discover that one of the gunners was too badly wounded to jump and the bombardier's parachute had been torn to shreds by enemy fire. Michael therefore stayed at the controls in the hope of saving these two crew members. The bombardier managed to jettison the incendiaries, and Michael brought the plane back to England where he crash-landed, even though the vacant belly turret had jammed with the guns pointing downward and neither the flaps nor the landing gear could be extended.

The only radio operator to win the award was Sergeant Forrest Vosler. Wounded by fire from fighters, he continued to man the machine gun mounted in his compartment until another 20-mm shell burst in the radio room, blinding him. He succeeded in repairing the damaged radio entirely by touch and sent out a distress signal when the plane went down at sea. After escaping from the wreckage, he remained with the other survivors until help arrived.

Besides Mathis, Michael and Vosler, the Eighth Air Force Medal of Honor winners were John Morgan, who eventually was shot down but survived the war; the four officers who fought at Ploesti, Addison Baker, John Jerstad and Lloyd Hughes—all killed—and Leon Johnson; William Lawley, who survived; Walter Truemper and Archibald Mathies, both of them killed; Leon Vance, killed in a plane crash en route back to the United States; Robert Femoyer, who refused a morphine injection because his navigational skill was needed; Donald Gott and William Metzger, killed trying to save a wounded crew member; Snuffy Smith and Frank Castle. The only person to win the Medal of Honor on his first mission was the irrepressible Smith. The highest ranking recipient was Castle, a brigadier general, whose posthumous award was the last earned by a member of the Eighth Air Force.

While demonstrating endurance and steady courage, the members of Eighth Air Force bomber units carried out the mission they had been assigned—conducting daylight precision attacks upon targets in Germany. Because the bombers could not wait for clear skies, the Norden sight yielded to H2X, and since radar was less accurate than the optical device, precision declined. Nevertheless, these men helped inflict crippling damage on key elements of German industry.

One industrial component, ball-bearing manufacture, took the heaviest blows delivered by the Eighth Air Force during 1943—the two Schweinfurt raids—without incurring lasting damage. At no time during the war did Speer's armament program falter because of ball-bearing shortages. Had the Allies during 1943 launched simultaneous attacks upon factories throughout the Reich that manufactured these devices, the result might have been different. Unfortunately, by the time the bomber forces were strong enough for such an undertaking, dispersal of plants, together with foreign purchases, had reduced the vulnerability of the ball-bearing industry.

Both the American strategic air forces and Britain's Bomber Command at times attacked the sources of ground strength. In November 1944 and again in March 1945, they hit towns and individual factories producing tanks and trucks and engines for these vehicles. The strikes, however, had little impact.

More successful were the attacks against the vengeance weapons. These blows delayed the buzz bombs until Allied armies had gained a lodgment on the continent of Europe. Germany's steel mills sustained heavy damage, and submarine construction yards proved infinitely more vulnerable than the massive pens upon which a great many bombs were wasted early in the war. Yet some submarine builders were fabricating steel sections for U-boat hulls as late as the spring of 1945. Damage to rail lines, however, prevented the enemy from shipping these components to assembly plants where the craft were to be completed and launched.

Attacks on German transportation proved effective, though inef-

"Precision" is the right term for
this stately B-17 formation

ficient in terms of tonnage required and number of targets that had to be struck. After D-Day Anglo-American bombers lavished almost a million tons of bombs on rail centers, marshaling yards and canals in the Balkans, northern Italy and Germany. The Eighth Air Force dropped some 235,000 tons, Fifteenth Air Force almost 150,000, Royal Air Force Bomber Command about 272,000; tactical aviation delivered the balance, roughly 300,000 tons. Although twisted rails and cratered roadbeds could be repaired easily, rolling stock became almost extinct, and the magnitude of the destruction proved overwhelming. In March 1945, for instance, as Allied troops were overrunning the Ruhr, aerial bombardment had cut all the rail lines serving this industrial region. Nor were rivers like the Danube and even North Sea coastal waters immune to aerial mines.

The German aviation industry presented an especially difficult target. Allied intelligence tended to underestimate the enemy's production capacity, much of it not fully used until 1944, and the ability of the aircraft plants to survive or avoid bombing. By making full use of all available machinery, installed at widely scattered sites to reduce vulnerability to attack, the Germans by the end of the war had created vast stockpiles of first-line aircraft that remained grounded for lack of fuel.

The oil offensive, championed by Spaatz, indeed proved decisive, though it took longer than he anticipated, in part because efforts were diverted against other types of targets. During the year following the initial oil attacks of April 1944, the Eighth Air Force dropped 70,000 tons of bombs on refineries and synthetic oil plants, the Fifteenth Air Force 60,000 tons and Bomber Command 90,000 tons. This same period saw German oil production decline by 95 percent.

Much of the analytical data on the role of air power in defeating Germany come from the 200 reports prepared immediately after the war by the U.S. Strategic Bombing Survey. During the spring of 1944, U.S. Army Air Forces had begun looking ahead to a postwar assessment of the effect of strategic bombing on Germany. Spaatz suggested the creation of a panel of civilian and military experts to carry out the work, Arnold agreed and the Joint Chiefs of Staff approved the idea. In September Franklin D'Olier, who headed the Prudential Life Insurance Company, took charge of the Strategic Bombing Survey, which had an authorized strength in excess of 1,000 military men and civilians. Operating from Frankfurt in conquered Germany, survey members interviewed military officers, bureaucrats, businessmen and technicians to elicit their views on the role of aerial bombardment in crushing Hitler's Reich.

On the basis of this testimony and examination of the devastation air power had caused, D'Olier's experts concluded that

> Allied air power was decisive in the war in western Europe. Hindsight inevitably suggests that it might have been employed differently or better in some respects. Nevertheless, it was decisive. In the air, its victory was complete; at sea, its contribution, combined with naval power, brought an end to the enemy's greatest naval threat—the U-boat; on land, it helped turn the tide overwhelmingly in favor of Allied ground forces. Its power and superiority made possible the success of the invasion. It brought the economy which sustained the enemy's armed forces to virtual collapse, although the full effects of this collapse had not reached the enemy's front lines when they were overrun by Allied forces. It brought home to the German people the full impact of modern war with all its horror and suffering. Its imprint on the German nation will be lasting.

This litany of accomplishments, however, suffered from a lack of participation by both the Russians and the British. Bomber Harris protested that the survey had slighted the contributions of his heavy bombers, and the American investigators acknowledged the difficulty of measuring precisely the impact of city busting on the morale, stamina and efficiency of German workers. All that the analysts could conclude was that production had continued even though workers were killed, driven from their homes and deprived of rest.

Despite 300,000 dead and more than twice that number injured, civilian morale did not crack. Yet the physical damage to the industrial centers often proved so severe that useful production was impossible. According to Speer, night raids against synthetic fuel plants inflicted worse damage than daylight raids. By the time the British joined the oil offensive, navigation aids could bring the massive Lancasters and Halifaxes precisely to the target. Whatever the objective, the Royal Air Force dropped a heavier weight of munitions than the Americans on a typical mission and, thanks to the use of a bomber stream instead of a more compact formation, dropped the bombs all night long, preventing firemen from going into action to check the raging flames.

The second weakness of the survey was its inability to measure the impact of the Soviet armed forces on Germany's economy. The Red Army overran refineries and coal mines, increased the burden on a transportation network already disrupted by bombing, forced the Germans to burn precious fuel and destroyed tanks, airplanes and men. Without Soviet cooperation, the Strategic Bombing Survey could not investigate this topic, nor could D'Olier's group determine the contribution made by the Eighth and Fifteenth Air Forces to the Russian advance.

Although conducted with skill and bravery, daylight precision bombing, as practiced by the men of the Eighth Air Force, had not defeated Germany. This form of warfare had, however, helped force the Third Reich to the brink of ruin. In spite of the tardy development of an escort fighter, American bombers had kept coming, attacking various el-

Allied air power choked German railroads.
Here, the Potsdam station in Berlin

No more speeches: the balcony where Hitler
often appeared

ements of German industry until they found categories of targets that
were vital to the enemy's survival. In short, the Eighth Air Force had
carried out the prewar concept of operations drawn up on the eve of war
by Harold George, Kenneth Walker, Laurence Kuter and Haywood
Hansell. Had the Eighth Air Force failed, had the courage of its airmen
broken, the goal of an independent American air arm could not have
been attained. But valor prevailed and the organization did succeed. On
18 September 1947, General Carl Spaatz took office as Chief of Staff of
the new U.S. Air Force.

In Context

This book has traced the story of the American daylight bombing of Germany from bases in England, and in telling this dramatic tale it has inevitably brought in the essential story of Allied strategic bombing in Europe. Certainly Britain's Bomber Harris has been a prominent member of the command cast along with the principal American leaders, and we have followed developments in British night bombing as well as those in the American daylight campaign. And details from the activities of the Italy-based U.S. Fourteenth Air Force have rounded out the story.

Strangely, American bombers might not have flown from stations in Britain had not the Japanese, on the other side of the world, attacked the naval base at Pearl Harbor and other U.S. installations in Oahu. Until 7 December 1941 the United States, though involved in the war and a neutral in name only, was the source of matériel and encouragement for Britain but was not directly engaged in the fighting.

The war had begun on 1 September 1939, when Adolf Hitler's German armies invaded Poland. Britain and France, then the Western Allies, were pledged to come to Poland's aid and did so to the extent of declaring war on Germany, though they rendered the Poles no other help. The German victory was swift. Then, after a winter dubbed the "Phony War," Hitler sent troops into Denmark, outwitted the Allies and seized Norway, and in May launched an invasion of the Low Countries and France. He was able to undertake these operations in the west because treaties of nonaggression and friendship with the Soviet Union had rendered Germany secure in the east; in fact, the two countries had divided Poland. In little more than a month the Battle of France was over and Hitler was master of the Continent. Britain stood alone, but the German panzers, which had awed the world, could not move on water. The air force would have to win control of the air over the island before the German Army could be ferried across the English Channel. There ensued the Battle of Britain, one of history's truly decisive battles. The Luftwaffe failed to break the Royal Air Force, and so the war in Europe would go on.

Balked, the German Führer turned his eyes again to the east, where his desires had always lain. In 1941, after a lightning sweep through the Balkans, the German Army—on June 22—unleashed Operation Barbarossa, the invasion of the Soviet Union. Britain and the United States quickly moved to extend material help to the Russians. The working principle was that whatever the ideology the Soviets professed, or whatever the arrangements they had only recently enjoyed with Nazi Germany, they were now enemies of the Führer and thus allies of the west.

Meanwhile, another expansionist military power was causing the United States deep apprehension. In Asia, Japan was building up what it called the "Greater East Asia Co-Prosperity Sphere," an extension of the Japanese Empire far to the south, to Burma, Indochina, Malaya and the Netherlands East Indies. This activity was not new. For years the Japanese had been nibbling at the great body of China, and since the summer of 1937 a full-scale war had been in progress.

The real fear in Washington was that Germany and Japan (and Italy, their junior partner in the Axis coalition) would move from conquest to conquest while committing no act of war against the United States, thus giving the Americans no specific reason to become active belligerents. This was also the fear in Britain, hard pressed and overextended.

But in one extraordinary week in December 1941 these fears vanished. Pearl Harbor was indeed an act of war against the United States, and Congress responded the next day with the appropriate declaration against Japan. Further, in the same week Hitler and Benito Mussolini declared war on the United States, though they were not bound to do so. The war was now truly global.

In accordance with previously agreed-upon strategy, the main American effort was initially directed to the war with Germany—the so-called Hitler-first strategy. This led to the building up of air strength in Britain, as told in *The Men Who Bombed the Reich*, and in November 1942 to the Anglo-American invasion of Northwest Africa, an area controlled by the Vichy French government, which was a captive of Hitler but a possible convert—or re-convert—to the Allied cause, at least in Africa.

Allied forces from the west moved in step with the British Eighth Army coming from Egypt, and in May 1943 the Axis had been driven out of Africa. Then came the invasions of Sicily and Italy and, in 1944, France, leading—together with the Soviet victories—to the downfall of the Third Reich.

Although the United States essentially pursued the Hitler-first strategy, signal victories came early in the Pacific—as is dramatically shown in *Carrier Victory*, another of the Men and Battle books. The Battle of the Coral Sea in May 1942 checked Japanese expansion southward, and it also revealed the shape of naval war to come. The chief weapons were aircraft, and the surface ships never exchanged a shot. In June, at Midway, the United States won a great carrier victory. This was the pivotal battle of the Pacific fighting, and thus one of the keys to the Allied victory in World War II. If, for example, Midway had gone against the United States, the Hitler-first principle might have been abandoned, or at least greatly diluted, because Americans would have had to defend—and probably unsuccessfully—Hawaii. And, certainly, U.S. forces could not have gone on the offensive in the Pacific in the summer of 1942, as they did at Guadalcanal in the Solomon Islands.

From that point on, the Americans pushed back the Japanese defensive perimeter, island to island—New Guinea, the Gilberts, the Marshalls, Saipan, Tinian, Guam—retaking the Philippines, reaching almost to the doorstep of Japan, at Okinawa in April 1945 (the bloody struggle for this island is recounted in the Men and Battle book called *Okinawa: The Great Island Battle*). The Imperial Japanese Navy was shattered, and most of the country's merchant fleet had been sunk by U.S. sub-

174

marines. American strategic bombers, waging a different kind of strategic air war from that in Europe, were incinerating Japan's cities.

But it still looked as though an Allied invasion of the Home Island would be necessary before the war could be ended. The prospect was one that appalled everybody who considered it. In August, however, the atomic bombs on Hiroshima and Nagasaki made the hopelessness of Japan's situation clear to all but a fringe of fanatics. There would be no invasion. There was instead, with surprising speed, peace.

For Further Reading

THE AIR MINISTRY, ASSISTANT CHIEF OF AIR STAFF (Intelligence). *The Rise and Fall of the German Air Force (1933–1945)*. London: The Air Ministry, 1948. A compact operational history of the Luftwaffe written from captured German documents for use at British Royal Air Force staff schools.

ARNOLD, H. H. *Global Mission*. New York: Harper, 1949. A discussion of events, loaded with personal anecdotes but revealing little about Arnold's personality or character.

COFFEY, THOMAS M. *Decision over Schweinfurt: The U.S. Eighth Air Force Battle for Daylight Bombing*. New York: David McKay, 1977. A splendid account of the great air battles of 1943, especially valuable because of the insights provided by General Ira Eaker and others.

CRAVEN, WESLEY FRANK, and CATE, JAMES LEA. eds. *The Army Air Forces in World War II*, vols. I, II, III, VI and VII. Chicago: University of Chicago Press, 1948–1958. Actually a collection of essays by a number of authors, including the two editors, the series suffers from unavoidable gaps. As the title indicates, the focus is almost exclusively American.

FREEMAN, ROGER A. *The Mighty Eighth: Units, Men, and Machines*. Garden City, N.Y.: Doubleday, 1970.

Written about men and machines, rather than plans and concepts, this is an excellent blending of personal narrative and combat report.

————. *Mustang at War*. Garden City, N.Y.: Doubleday, 1974.

Although mainly a picture book, it contains valuable information on the development and early deployment of this decisive weapon.

GOLDBERG, ALFRED. "General Carl A. Spaatz," in Field Marshal Sir Michael Carver, ed. *The War Lords: Military Commanders of the Twentieth Century*. Boston: Little, Brown, 1976.

A brief sketch of a man that Eisenhower considered one of his outstanding generals, emphasizing the mutual confidence shared by the two officers.

GREEN, WILLIAM. *War Planes of the Second World War: Fighters*, vol I. Garden City, N.Y.: Doubleday, 1960.

Details the development of Luftwaffe fighters from the eve of the war until the advent of the jet.

HANSELL, HAYWOOD S., JR. *The Air Plan That Defeated Hitler*. Atlanta: Haywood Hansell, 1972.

Offers a fascinating glimpse into planning on the eve of World War II.

HASTINGS, DONALD W., WRIGHT, DAVID G., and GLUECK, BERNARD C. *Psychiatric Experiences of the Eighth Air Force: First Year of Combat, July 4, 1942–July 4, 1943*. New York: Josiah Macy, Jr., Foundation, 1944.

Reveals problems that persisted long after 4 July 1943.

INFIELD, GLENN B. *The Poltava Affair: A Russian Warning, An American Tragedy*. New York: Macmillan, 1973.

A detailed account of the shuttle bombing effort, using bases in Russia, written from a cold war perspective.

JABLONSKI, EDWARD. *Flying Fortress: The Illustrated Biography of the B-17s and the Men Who Flew Them*. Garden City, N.Y.: Doubleday, 1965.

Especially valuable for information on the development and early use of the B-17.

PEASLEE, BUDD J. *Heritage of Valor: The Eighth Air Force in World War II*. New York: J. B. Lippincott, 1964.

An eyewitness account of operations during 1943, with a brief summary of subsequent fighting.

PRICE, ALFRED. *Luftwaffe Handbook, 1939–1945*. New York: Charles Scribner's Sons, 1977.

A successful basic reference manual, especially good in its treatment of antiaircraft defenses.

ROBERTSON, BRUCE, ed. *United States Army and Air Force Fighters, 1916–1961*. Fallbrook, Calif.: Aero Publishers, 1961.

Contains some interesting detail about American fighters of World War II.

SPEER, ALBERT. *Inside the Third Reich*, Richard and Clara Winston, tr. New York: Macmillan, 1970.

The memoirs of the wartime director of the German armaments program, whose "idealized" view of Hitler at the time somehow overlooked the enormity of the Führer's crimes.

THOMAS, LOWELL, and JABLONSKI, EDWARD. *Doolittle: A Biography*. Garden City, N.Y.: Doubleday, 1976.

Filled with anecdotes, this book tries to describe a man who was adventurer and technician, business executive and military leader.

VERRIER, ANTHONY. *The Bomber Offensive*. New York: Macmillan, 1968.

An excellent account of the techniques employed and issues resolved during the Anglo-American bomber offensive against Germany.

WEBSTER, SIR CHARLES, and FRANKLAND, NOBLE. *The Strategic Air Offensive against Germany, 1939–1945*, 4 vols. London: Her Majesty's Stationery Office, 1961.

Easily the best treatment of a complicated topic, it emphasizes planning but also covers operations and technology.

Index

180

181

183

184

THE MEN WHO BOMBED THE REICH

Bernard C. Nalty
Carl Berger

1942—American flyers and their bombers were coming to Europe. Their mission: along with the British, bomb the Third Reich into surrender. Their method: daylight precision attack.

But the Royal Air Force had already tried daylight bombing and abandoned it. RAF veterans said that it was too costly in men and planes. Even the B-17—the Flying Fortress, its proud crews called it—would, the British said, prove dangerously vulnerable to German antiaircraft defenses. The British bombed by night.

Could the confident Americans, trained in the clear skies of the southern and southwestern United States, carry out their daylight doctrine amid the clouds and storms of northern Europe and in the teeth of German flak and fighters? Could they penetrate to the heart of the Reich without their own fighter escorts?

The Men Who Bombed the Reich takes you on the missions that tried to answer these questions—from the first flights over occupied western Europe to the savage battles over targets like Regensburg and Schweinfurt, where the attackers' losses ran as high as 15 percent (a rate that could wipe out the U.S. Eighth Air Force).

How the problem was solved is a key part of the story this book tells. But there is much more: acts of incredible heroism over Ploesti and other far-flung targets; the massive raids of the "Big Week"; the working of the plan that helped the 1944